THE ONE TECHNIQUE

THE ONE TECHNIQUE

LEARN HOW 20% OF MINDFULNESS LEADS TO 80% OF SUCCESS IN LIFE

HyA HARRY ALEXANDER

www.harryalexander.in

Notion Press

Old No. 38, New No. 6
McNichols Road, Chetpet
Chennai - 600 031

First Published by Notion Press 2017

ISBN 978-1-947988-15-6

Thank You

My sincere thanks to Life itself from which this book is inspired.

This book would not be possible if it was not for my wife Jovita who held on to me when I was struggling. She sees something in me, which even I don't see at times.

My deep gratitude to V Shetty and his family who bestowed me with their love and care during the five days of intense editing that I undertook at their serene abode in Manglaore.

I express hearfelt gratitude to my entire family who have been with me on this journey.

I am grateful to my book launch team and all my reviewers.

My sincere thanks to Ashok Kumar Ranganathan, Yogesh Karawade; and Anil Varghese, for their earnest and endearing support by funding my passionate endeavour.

This book is dedicated to my wife Jovita and children Ethan and Faith.

– Harry Alexander

Contents

Praise for
The One Technique: Reviews

"Life is about finding a purpose. And the ones who have found a purpose become an inspiration to others. Such people are angles on earth - slowly and softly guiding others to find a purpose in their lost lives. Harry Alexander's book - The One technique is such a book from where you can find a purpose for your life. Starting with a personal journey Harry narrates how life can seem successful yet is actually in a mess and the means to come out of this mess. The book talks about meditation and its method to find oneself. The power of being with oneself and the techniques to reach there. The inner joinery starts with oneself and ends in oneself. You too can explore the journey through this book. Remember, this book is not about reading. It is about reading and then practising all that you have read. Have a great journey through meditation to discover yourself...Best wishes"

Dr. Radhakrishnan Pillai, Deputy Director, Chanakya International Institute of Leadership Studies (CIILS), University of Mumbai,
Author - Corporate Chanakya, Chanakya's 7 secrets of leadership, Chanakya in You, Katha Chanakya, Chanakya in daily life, Inside Chanakya's mind - Aanvikshiki and the art of thinking

The author tries to contemprorize the ancient Indian wisdom in an amazing way. He has wisely shown the mind-body integrity, a key quest in philosophy as a discipline across the world and its relevance for achieving eternal peace. This book removes the merely ascetic image of Indian spiritual science and establishes its relevance to day to day life of a common man. The famous Einsteinian formula of 'E = MC^2' is paraphrased as 'Enlightenment = Mindfulness + Consciousness^2' which shows great insight of the author. The author has evolved a perfect model suitable to contemporary lifestyle from the archaic science of vipassana. Today's man has included so many new things in his daily lifestyle but has forgotten to factor in the real key of eternal joy. The author helps one find that key and gives a model which can easily be implemented by anyone in his daily routine. This book beautifully captures that however the world advances on technology front, India has a treasure of eternal wisdom which she can offer to the world.'

Dr. Harish Navale, Assistant Professor,
Department of Philosophy,
Savitribai Phule University of Pune

'If you ask me to categorize The One Technique as per the style of writing (a traditional way of classification of literature) I would say that it is both a story and a DIY guide book. Harry starts this book with his story and slowly pulls you in his narrative with rightly placed, small, key exercises. The powerful dialogue which he establishes with his readers through this style of writing instantly brings the reader to the "NOW" and then gently takes him or her on an introspection ride. Harry narrates, explains, asks his readers to reflect but he also offers pearls of his own distilled wisdom spread across the book in the form of various punches like 'released to serve' rather than 'released from service' or 'what you teach, you strengthen in yourself' etc. The beauty of this book is that it is a narration of 'introspection' moving towards better clarity about oneself in which the author becomes the alter ego of the reader and eventually this duality too fades away and you are left with better understanding about your own self.'

Prachi Moghe, Freelance Editor and Translator (Paramarsh, Indian Philosophical Quarterly)

'The One Technique' is a beginners guide that amalgamates western concepts with Indian mediation techniques allowing the reader to be a participant rather than a recipient of the joys of mediation and life changing scenarios that emerge through self-connections with the mind, body and soul."

Mr. Aashay Abhyankar, Mentor, Abhyankars IAS Academy

"The One Technique is a great lesson for everyone. It explains the process of self-discovery through meditation in simple words. The book will guide us for spiritual as well as material success by explaining how the two need not be necessarily antagonistic. As a practitioner of meditation myself, my take away from the book is this very insight that the author very effectively puts across."

Dr. Varadraj Bapat, Professor, Shailesh J Mehta School of Management, IIT Mumbai

All through my experiences, I have come across many people who indeed required certain mentorship to help them overcome the challenges posed by life, most of which were rather perceived than real. Sometimes our own imagination eclipses the reality and this indiscriminate use of imagination creates, more often than not, a sense of falsehood and entraps our lives. Harry Alexander was very rightful, thoughtful and mindful in relating his experiences to these so called 'imaginative realities' helping the readers way to figure for themselves and work their way out of it.

Before giving this review, I met Harry Alexander multiple times to understand the thoughts behind this book. The more I spoke to him, I realized that the more I understood this book, and the more I read this book, the more I understood him. This book is straight from his heart, sweat, life. Like 'Walking the Talk' in life, this book is 'Writing the Walk' of life.

Like a surgeon who uses his precision tools so skillfully yet mindfully, so deftly yet delicately to address the pain points, Harry's insights in the book will help the readers through a thorough experience in understanding their real pain points and offers a technique everyone can follow throughout their life.

I strongly recommend that *The One Technique* is the one technique" everyone should try. For everyone who are looking for ways to transform their lives though actionable insights, this 'read it once, reap the benefits for ever' kind of a book will be an enabler.

A good weekend read for a whole weekday's practice, all the weeks.

Srikanth Kumar Kota
Project Management Evangelist, Author, Founder, CEO - Nucleus Consulting Group

"*The One Technique* is the story of the transformation of Harry Alexander. The conversational style of writing, the humour and the engaging content coupled with my own active imagination took me on a ride with the author through his experiences.

Harry's journey has seen the highs with the lows like a Hollywood action adventure. In the current market scenario, many of us may have experienced job loss or felt threatened by anxiety for our jobs much like Harry did. And this stress percolates to all areas of life, straining relationships, health and finances. Can we be inspired by Harry's story where instead of going on a downward spiral of anxiety, despair and hopelessness, he chose to use the same circumstances to propel him to awareness through meditation? Through this path of mindfulness he transformed his life to a life of giving; a life of service — a life of living his passion of coaching people to observe themselves, accept themselves and become aware of their own significant purpose in life."

V Shetty
Co-Founder, A Kube; and marketing expert
Pune, India

"The credibility of this book is more when we see the author looking into the reservoir of our heritage and bringing out pearls of wisdom without any prejudice of culture, ethnicity, believe, religion. He does not talk about his way. He discuss his journey and of how he learnt, walked, faltered and learnt again or reacted faster to situations so that he could salvage with all his might where many of us are too proud or ignorant to accept or even believe that such a situation exists.

This book is an extensive work of labour, where the author does not create a myth but quotes extensively from various sources; his thought process is crystal clear.

Harry Alexander is candid in telling the readers that he has faced similar issues or battled the same bulge and baggage in both the literary and figurative sense, the obsession with work, mild alcoholism or living in the smug arrogance of feeling invincible; and what happened when he suddenly lost his job?

Harry Alexander looks and provides a gateway to a holistic process of healing and management through Vipassana and draws out a time table for people like us and how to go about it.

This book caters to anyone who buys a list of self-help books and gives up mid-way. *The One Technique* tells us — "Wait, if you have read it all, I have something up my sleeve, which will have you take up and follow a few routines." This is worth serious reading. Cheers and Congrats!"

Ranjai Ghosh
Ex-Professor of Economics, Marketing.
Researcher, Symbosis (Pune); IIM (Cal)

"A book which will guide you in some way or the other in your spiritual as well as material journey. Good work, Harry."

Saurabh Chavan
Author, *The journey of my life to happiness and beyond*

The One Technique is a lesson in real-life situations. As Harry travels through the tough times in life it reminds me of what Bruce Lee had said, "Take things as they are — Punch when you have to punch. Kick when you have to kick."

It's a growing process; and rising from the situation by understanding the basics of life.

I have read a lot about positivity in the past. But the newness of *The One Technique* is explaining the process of mindfulness. As Harry has said rightly, we know through these theories how a fruit should look like, taste like, feel like, and smell like. But what we miss is that we have never tasted the fruit, so we get lost in the search for it. Harry will guide you to find this link through his journey.

Diana Pais,
Sr. Sales Manager,
Star Health & Allied Insurance Co. Ltd.
Pune

Introduction

Happiness is not the end; it's the journey

It is not necessary to give up everything, run to the mountains and give up a life among people to be happy, liberated and content. The universe is in a hurry of sorts to get more and more people to realise themselves and live a life of service. The best part is you can continue to be healthy, wealthy and have enriching relationships as you continue to serve. Maybe instant messaging (IM) technology has caught up with the universe or it's the other way round; a gift from the universe's for us to know that things are on the move in the galaxy a bit faster now.

If you want to align yourself with the universe's ever-expanding nature and be part of the revolution, which is the expansion of your consciousness, you can use the one technique that makes all the difference — Mindfulness.

Meditation forms an integral part of mindfulness. You don't have to wait to find enlightenment or even for years of wisdom to build or to reap the benefits, nor do you have to struggle, suffer, self-mortify, and flagellate yourself anymore. You don't even have to give up your luxuries to be happy. As you start using this technique of mindfulness that has always been around, but thought to be the domain of spiritual mystics and yogi's for a long time. It is now yours to learn and use too. Just by taking this one step, your present lifetime will be a happy one; and guess what! You can always be pleasantly surprised and be enlightened — here and now — by realising the deeper truth.

80% of the most successful people interviewed by Tim Ferris for the book *Tools of Titans* meditate in some form. If you are not a Titan yet, you can be. The one thing you can start towards being mindful is by paying attention. To learn to pay attention, the best tool is to meditate. It is not hocus pocus, abracadabra stuff. It is just science.

Through meditation you can actually harness the Pareto Principle for better living. Economist Vilfredo Pareto's 80/20 rule states that efforts as small as 20% can lead to 80% of results. It is basically a rule of inequality, which means that the majority of your creation, abundance and happiness come from the minor efforts that you put in. The most significant effort that can boost your success to 80% is being mindful. So, without getting plastered to the numbers of 80/20, simply start investing 20% of your time being mindful and observe the change.

Before we jump right into the 'How to' part of it, here is a little something on the book. Like most things we do — yes, right; most things, not ALL — there is a purpose. This book too has a purpose. And like most simple things that cannot be explained easily, you begin by stating what you cannot do. So, I will begin by stating what the purpose of this book is not. The purpose is not to get you enlightened or promise you that I have what it takes to get you there. I too am a fellow traveller. It is not to make you live based on what I have learnt or experienced. Yes, you are right! No one can get you to live as per their experience and learning, even though most people try hard to do this. It is also not to get a profound message out. It is rather to learn along with you. If I have used the second person 'you', it is to address the reader directly. This does not indicate that I know better or I am separate from you, the reader. It is quite the opposite. It is to look at myself from your perspective and gather the many pieces of the puzzle that make ME, but are also in you, and make a sincere effort to put it together. It is one of my efforts in my quest to find more about myself. In doing so, I have an intention that you too can pause for a little moment, notice where you are in life and maybe awaken ever so lightly that the light of dawn creeps into your eyes, and maybe… just maybe… you wake up to the glorious day ahead of you .

What it does have, is a story. I would love to call it an 'inspirational memoir', but I will leave that to you to label. If you are inspired in some way, I will add the word inspirational. For now, it is a memoir. Maybe if I can point you even one step in the path to self-realisation and develop the habit of creating a fuller life, then this book will achieve its purpose. The story takes 5 of the most intimate threads of my life and weaves them through the fabric of life. The intimate threads being:

The mind and its ability to create.

Relationships and their teaching.

Health and its ever-changing pattern and how your mindfulness will boost your health.

How to attain financial stability to lead an abundant life.

Finally, and not the least of all, is the act of service; how to live your passions and serve.

One of the peripheral insights that I would probably like for this book to prompt is for you to think about starting a personal intimate project — A self-happiness project. In a way, like a start-up, as explained by Eric Reis in his book *The Lean Start Up*. Here, the start-up is not a business or an IT project but something very elemental, very foundational; and the sooner one uses the tools available, tests them and realises if they work or not, the better it is; not only for the person concerned, but for the people around — why! The universe itself! If this step is not producing results, then a pivot is in order. Pivot towards the next thing that works to make your project a success. It is my personal experience that meditation is a powerful tool; it is a place through which miracles happen. Like different apps offering the same service, you have various method and techniques offering the same service. I have experienced Vipassana meditation as one of the powerful techniques by virtue of its scientific foundation. Trying it out as soon as possible without any delay is a sure-fire way of proving its efficacy. So, get on with it and get yourself to a meditation centre the first chance you get.

A little bit on the structure of the book. It is written for those of you who have a spark within, however not aware of what that spark means as yet. It is designed to offer the power of the one technique, which is meditation, to all those who want to overcome their inner resistances and achieve a happy and successful life. It does not provide just one tool or technique; although I personally use the Vipassana technique to be mindful. You could use any technique that suits you to become mindful. Mindfulness is the key that opens doors to a world which cannot be seen, but still exists.

I share my journey of evolving spiritually in the most insistent reality called the world. It is about my journey of how I have used mindfulness as the single most powerful tool to harness the potential of my subconscious mind.

The book has three sections

Section 1 takes you into the portal called NOW. Being fully here and now is one of the most practical and easy ways to step into the zone of oneness with life. It is a portal that is always staring us in the face, yet we fail to see it. This section gives you a chance to assess where you are in relation to the present moment and sets the tone and pace to move to the next level of where you want to be.

Section 2 deals with continuing on the path of being mindful of this moment; you are taken into understanding that nothing is permanent. It is all temporary and passing. You realise that this impermanence is also applicable to your life and the habits, beliefs and concepts that you hold on to so dearly. If everything is changing, why not change to be better?

The world as we see it is an extension of our own minds. When one knows that the mind is manifesting and creating their realities based on our thoughts, you wake up from your dream state. To wake up, your body plays a vital role. The body is the portal into your mind. When the mind and body are in sync, miracles happen. You too can work these miracles.

Section 3 explains the situation where you know what you know; and to use the mind instead of the mind using you to develop and maintain relationships that nourish you. You will mindfully live in a state of gratitude, acting out the purpose that life has intended for you. With the awareness of the impermanence, and experiencing that only 'Now' is all that matters, you start seeing better health and manage your wealth wisely. You will learn to be of this world and yet not of this world

This is a science experiment. It is based on sound scientific experiments which were conducted 2500 years ago and then forgotten for a long time. Now is your chance to jump in and activate that inquisitive nature within you to align science with the intangible, unseen world where miracles are the normal order of business. This really could be the one turning point you have been waiting for.

Now that you know what is in store, let's begin the journey from where it started for me

SECTION 1

THE PORTAL IS OPEN. IT IS NOW

Going Pear Shaped

I was living the life of a workaholic and a mild alcoholic, if there is such a state of being. I thrived on the concept "if you don't smoke like a chimney and drink like a fish you cannot be trusted." Being in The Navy and then later in the oil and gas industry, smoking and drinking seemed to be the norm, and the group dynamics in the office and offshore on the vessels/ships is determined by your smoking and drinking habits.

Another common phrase I also kept hearing was, "this is going pear shaped"; and this was not at the company or project level, but for the industry I was in. I was aware of the massive job losses and pay cuts people were receiving across the oil and gas industry. There were strong rumours that there would be layoffs at my company too.

So, when my life started going pear-shaped, I should not have been surprised; but there I was, totally shocked! It was the proverbial 'deer caught in the headlights' scene. Here is what happened — I was sitting at my desk with the assumed gumption that I had a very secure job, even considering that the industry was going south. This confidence was due to the fact that I was always told by my peers and my superiors that the portfolio I was handling was unique and would not be made redundant. So, when the CEO knocked on my door saying, "let's talk," I was taken by surprise because I was not expecting this knock so early on. Well, after 7 years of active duty, to use the Navy term, I was let go. Just like that I was jobless in a foreign country.

With hindsight and three years of time below the bridge, I can say that being terminated from a job which I loved and enjoyed was good. It was a turning point. But at the time it happened it was a hard blow. Being a foreigner and working overseas has its benefits, but you don't want to be there when you get fired and without a job. Fortunately for me, I had saved some money to live and take care of my young family.

We had a saying in the Navy: "Tough times don't last, but tough people do." It was to build the character of the officers and the soldiers so that they could see through tough times. For me being laid off with a young family was one such tough time. Interestingly, there was a corollary to the saying developed by the cadre: "When the going gets tough, the tough report sick." So, here I was, in the midst of a crisis with a choice to stand up and see through the time and use it to my benefit or go down under and report sick. You guessed it right! If I am here writing about it, then I have survived the episode. How I survived is what makes it interesting and the life lessons that started during that phase of my life have been leading me on to some amazing experiences. One of the key lessons that led me on my new career as a life coach/trainer/mentor/author was the lesson of being present in the moment. *The Power of Now* was the one book that made a huge impact on my life at that point in time.

When I look back at the entire time frame as a movie, I saw patterns. It went something like this — drinking issues; the loss of a loved one; making money, but every now and then awakening ever so lightly to observe that one thought, "Am I doing enough? Am I living my passion?" Then, losing a job followed by a generous shower of misunderstandings with one of the most important people in life, my wife. To put it simply, we were not bonding as we should have been, considering that we had come together for a combined effort towards a spiritual evolution.

When I started going deeper into understanding the power of the present moment, major shifts occurred. I call them major, again, by hindsight. At that point in time it was sheer hard work, stress and negativity and arguments. Gradually, I saw some change. In a way, it is like waking Up; or going to rehab and being sober after a long period of being unaware under the influence of alcohol.

This turning point and the new phase saw me giving up my quest for self-annihilation through booze. I noticed that my wife was one of the most influential teachers that was sent into my life just before my mom passed away. I awakened just long enough to see that money was not everything to be happy in life, even though it did not hurt to have enough of it lasting a lifetime. I also realised that labels are not essential to make a difference for others, at times they are obstacles instead of any help. Serving others seems like one of the most satisfying endeavours I can undertake. Of course, the teachings of our modern gurus keep stating that when you do what you love, money will follow. I know it is true, just that it has not started showing up in my life yet.

As I kept searching and looking for deeper realisation, I could sense a guiding force leading me towards new ventures and a different lifestyle. My thirst to become intimate with the present moment was insatiable. For some reason I was hooked to the concept of 'inner body experience' which Eckhart Tolle mentioned in *The Power of Now*. Being an engineer and wanting logical answers, I read as many books as my new job allowed me, to understand this experience. I researched techniques to get a thorough experience of this moment. Through one of the searches I stumbled on the Vipassana technique of meditation. Soon, I found myself on a hill in Penang. It was here that another new path opened up — The Path into the MIND. It was no longer outside in. It changed to inside out. This is the starting point where the realisation that the mind is all hit home. And if the mind is all, then the fullness of this mind can be used to create a life of service and abundance through mindfulness. The technique of mindfulness can be learnt through the art of meditation.

STARTING POINT:
Just Breathe

JUST BREATHE and BE AWARE OF IT. This is it!

This is how I started getting intimate with life itself. Simple? You are not going to buy this, are you; that the simplicity of living a beautiful life is breathing and being aware of it? Our conditioning does not allow us to believe and accept simple phenomenon. We are used to complex problems, complicated life situations, and out of the world problems. It is unacceptable that life is waiting simply around the corner of the next aware breath that you take.

Well, what if I quoted the Bible: "Be still and Know I am God." This is too much to accept as well. You will question the Bible too for its simplicity. The fact is that this is where you lose the battle even before you start. There is one action which is required of you to start the process. Just believe that doing nothing, being still, and simply breathing are all that is required for you to know God, to communicate with life and be happy and successful.

Now, follow these simple steps...

1. Sit comfortably.
2. Notice that you are breathing.
3. Pay attention to your natural respiration.

4. Be aware of every breath that comes in.
5. Be aware of every breath that comes out.

Do this for 10 breaths! On completion, open your eyes and keep sitting. This is what I found myself doing for 10 days at the hill on Penang where life took me. This was in response to my search to understand inner body awareness as mentioned by Tolle.

Step 1 of the process is the simplest of all — Become aware of the natural respiration. I did this over days, and the last couple of years I have been practising it

At the Vipassana centre at Penang I did this on a demanding schedule. It's funny actually; the demanding schedule is not for creating, but to become aware of the breathing. The simple act of becoming aware is a path to liberation.

The sessions were as follows:

04.30–06.30 - 2 hrs

08.00–09.00 - 1 hr

09.00–11.00 - 1 hr

13.00–14.30 - 1.5 hr

14.30–17.00 - 2.5 hr

18.00–19.00 - 1 hr

19.00–20.30 - 1.5 hr

20.30–21.00 - 1.5 hr

Doing this period of time, life started letting me in on some of its secrets hiding in plain sight. Once you start becoming aware of your breath, you realise that this is where everything is! The present moment. Only here and now. The question that arises then is, why be here at all? Why don't we live in the past or continue living in the future?

Why be here at all?

Where can you be if not here and now?

Imagine this scenario — This day and age where instant gratification is the way of life; where fight and flight responses are being taken to newer, higher proportions; stress is an accepted term and used as a way of greeting in many responses — for instance, you ask your colleague or friend how they are, do you even get surprised to hear them tell you it's all stressful? I sometimes feel that people feel guilty if they don't have stress. Nothing good or bad about it. It just is. Stress is caused by imaginary problems created by the mind. These are mostly about the future with questions like, "What If I lose my job? What if I lose my money? How can I survive through an ordeal of losing a loved one?" It goes on and on. On the other hand, the past comes to haunt you. Don't you remember the failures that you had? The loss you suffered? There is a constant, repetitive loop being played out in the mind. We lose 80% of our mind power through this process. When you are so occupied by your imaginary future or a terrible past, how can you be available for life to make contact with you?

If you want to create something beautiful and live abundantly instead of living a life dictated by future circumstances, other people and past failures, you might want to get in touch with life and open channels of communications with life itself.

The medium of communication which life uses to communicate with is through the present moment. This moment is the most accessible portal, so to say, where life interacts with us. It cannot happen to us in the past or the future.

You might notice that communication is the forefront of technological advances. Every day, there are new developments in the way we communicate with each other. We have numerous apps to make our life easier through communication. If communication between us is so critical and considered the backbone of success, then how important is it for us to be in constant touch with life? As we use these numerous apps, softwares and technologies to communicate among ourselves, life uses the present moment as a means and mode to make us fully available to create a life that we want.

Marianne Williamson puts if beautifully in her book *Law of Divine Compensation*. "The Only time that God's time intersects with linear time is in the present moment. Miracles happen not in the past or the future but in the Now."

As I mentioned earlier in the introduction, my life situations changed in terms of complexity for the better once I made contact with life by being available in the present. If you want to, you too can experience this change. You have to show up for it, that's all. How can you show up? First, find out where you are and that is a start.

When was the last time you took stock of your awareness of the present moment? If it's been a while, let's take you through a simple assessment to get your 'present moment awareness' score.

ACTION #1 Your Awareness Scale Assessment

Are you living here and now? The present moment is all there is for life to unfold. One cannot live anywhere but the present.

You need to understand why living in the present moment is important; develop the mindset to live from that space, use the tools to create the path now and set up a way to consistently follow through to a fulfilling and abundant life

... And you DON'T have to work hard, just BE.

To get into that gap of the present moment through your own potential, use this assessment tool. This assessment is focused on the present and will give you an idea of your awareness right now. Please complete all items. Rate each item on a scale of 1–5. Choose the one score that best represents your feelings, thoughts and behaviour. Choose how true each statement is for you.

1	2	3	4	5
Less True				More True

#No	Statement	Response (1–5)
1	I think of the future very often. There is a marathon of thoughts running in my head about the future.	
2	I like to think of the past. The thoughts of my past take up a major part of my thinking time and energy.	
3	I spend more time thinking about the past and future.	
4	I have experienced moments of 'no thoughts'.	
5	I question myself, "what would happen if I stopped thinking?"	
6	I practice meditation.	
7	I sit quietly and observe my thoughts and sensations once a day at least for 10 minutes.	
8	I have experienced moments of clear intuition and taken action based on that intuition.	
9	I know my top 5 passions.	
10	I have created intentions to match my top 5 passions.	
11	I know that the intentions are made in the present moment.	

#No	Statement	Response (1–5)
12	The idea of someone supporting and guiding me through my Intention-setting is very intriguing to me.	
13	I am willing to explore the possibility of creating my life as per my intentions.	
14	I believe that lifelong learning and self-improvement is a virtue that I have.	
15	I notice that there are important areas in my life that seem out of balance and I am willing to work to set up a balance.	
16	I could use assistance in identifying my top 5 passions.	
17	I know and feel that now I am ready to explore ways of developing myself (personally and professionally).	
18	I trust that the universe is directing me towards living fully now.	
19	If asked to write down 3 major changes that I would like to make in my life over The next 3 months, I would have no problem answering.	
20	I have a strong desire to make my life simpler.	
23	I am a strong person and dedicate time, energy and finances to identify changes required and to implement them.	

25	I am keen to live life more fully and abundantly.	
26	I am interested in exploring how the present moment is the most important step. That is required to start living fully here and now.	
27	I usually challenge predetermined and conditioned ways of Thinking, which are not aligned to my development.	
28	I am not looking to solve or reduce any disorders like anxiety; instead I am keen to promote personal development.	

Score Interpretation

Total Score 91–150

This score indicates a high likelihood that you are living in the moment and are willing to explore the benefits of your self-awareness. You are living a life aligned to life's purpose. You are likely to be someone who has experienced the power of the present moment and understand that self-awareness and living in the now opens up the doorway to just 'BE'. You could significantly benefit from going deeper into this realm and attend a structured meditation course to keep experiencing life fully in the present moment, identify your passions and develop the intentions aligned with life's plans.

Your ability to stay focused on taking specific steps to help yourself meet your goals is likely to help you gain a great deal from the meditation process. The ideal time to take this step to take is now and you should take advantage of your knowing and intuition.

Total Score 46–91

This score indicates a high likelihood that you have experienced the power of living in the moment, albeit fleeting, and would like to explore further. You do see the little light and are waking up. The chances are that your experiences are fleeting. However, the seed for that space of being is planted within your mind; and if you continue exploring your inner realisation, you will come to a point in life where lessons, teachers and resources will be made available by the universe.

Total Score 0–45

Your answers are not consistent with someone who is living in the moment or intending to live in the moment. It is likely that you are not experiencing any of life's subtle directions at the moment. This may be because you are not familiar of the power available to each moment; and also, you may not be aware that this power could be experienced simply by starting your own happiness project and giving time for yourself. Once you become more aware, you could harness the power of the universal intelligence towards creating and manifesting an abundant life.

Disclaimer: *This assessment is not intended to provide a psychological or psychiatric diagnosis and your completion of the test does not indicate a professional or medical counselling by the administrator of the test.*

NOW THAT YOU ARE HERE…

Take time out. Sit down in one place and pay attention to your surroundings; to the way you are seated.

Recognise the present habits that you use.

What time do you wake up?

What time do you sleep?

How many times do you brush your teeth each day?

What are the predominant thoughts that you have through the day?

What are you deeply convinced about?

Are there any old habits that you wish you did not have? It could be a habit of sleeping late into the morning or the habit of being distracted.

Which old habit do you want to overwrite with a new habit?

Go through your entire day and notice how you are living the day.

It is a well-established fact that writing down your thoughts is a concrete way of starting on this journey. Thought gains clarity when written down, and is the first step towards manifesting a new reality. It is an essential practice for moving forward.

As you start becoming mindful you will realise that there is something holding you back; you might not be able to name what it is. As you delve deeper into the awareness of the present moment by focusing on your respiration or using the body and its sensations; the inner and outer body, you will come face to face with your bondages. Now, what can you do about them and how?

As the intensity of your focus becomes sharper, you might face a revelation, as I did. I got my revelation standing in front of a small waterfall on a hill at Penang. "Harry, you don't have to think to be alive." I was stumped! Till now I had given complete control to the mind and it was running my life. What life was revealing to me was to understand that mind was a good tool when used by you, but when it takes control, you have lost it. Do you agree that you don't have be think to be alive? Have you experienced what it is to be aware of being alive without thoughts?

So, the very first secret revealed to me, which again is hiding in plain sight, is that the MIND IS ALL.

Mind Is All

"The mind precedes all phenomenon."

– Gotama, The Buddha

The mind is all. It is in the mind that we all exist. Mind can be anywhere, everywhere and take any form. Think of it like the air we breathe. It can be subtle, calm and subdued one moment and the next moment it has kicked up a storm of immense proportions. It is in the mind that thoughts take shape, and given enough attention, these thoughts become things. What it implies is that you can create physical realities by the power of your mind by using the tool of paying attention to the thoughts. At times it's a mind-bend though to realise that the Mind uses itself to know more and evolve.

Being a mechanical engineer I have seen computers that drive numerically-controlled lathes, robots, and high-precision machines. Now, think of the computer that is driving the machines. If you imagine the mind to be a computer, the programs running in the computer are like the thoughts we have. Now, if this computer is used to run a numerically-controlled machine, then it is the programs that determine the effort, quality and speed with which the machine operates. So, these programs deliver results, don't they? The quality and type of the program determine the output. If you run old, worn-out programs that compromise quality, are slow, have some code missing, can you expect a high quality end product from the machine? Liken the machine to your body here just as a simple analogy. If your programs are to be lazy, find excuses, etc., then the output will be same as the programs. Now, if you have to change the output of the machine, what would have to be done first? Change the machines or the programs or the mind?

We all have some old programs or the other running in our mind, and most often, we might not be aware of them. Yet, we wake up each day expecting different results from the actions we take. Energy is being drained away to run unwanted, old programs, which are constantly running behind the screen. Here, think of your mobile phone; there are numerous background apps running in the background that you cannot even see on the screen, yet they consume battery power and if allowed to run for a long time, your phone will just be useless.

If you want to be of service, be useful and live a life of purpose, it is vital that you take stock of the old programs that are running in your mind. These programs are your habit patterns. Observe and notice what you are creating around you. Are you a force of love? Do you influence people around you to live a full life? Or do they feel drained when you are around them? Do you have peace and contentment, or are you always anxious and depressed?

If you want to change, you cannot start by asking for a change of the machine; instead, start from changing the old patterns. It is difficult to break old patterns. They need to be dissolved, really, but it is a much more difficult task to break them; rather, it is easier to create new programs which are aligned with life's purpose. In creating new patterns, you don't spend time and energy trying to break something; rather, from the word go you start creating and this action automatically dissolves the old stubborn program.

So, how does this reprogramming occur? How can you create a new habit pattern? These are the two questions that are answered in this chapter by establishing that mind precedes all phenomenon.

There are 3 precepts and two actions, which when used consistently and diligently, bring about a major shift in perception. And as the course in Miracles says, "Miracles rearrange perception and place the levels of perception in true perspective." This rearranging of perception comes about as you sit and learn to be still, quite literally actually.

It is not easy to be still and quiet and sit doing nothing. The present mindset has been that of multitasking, of being busy doing something all the time and the assumption is that if you are busy enough doing a lot most of the time you will find that elusive success, happiness, peace and tranquillity. If you have been a doer, you will know what I mean.

It requires a change in perspective to realise that it is exactly the opposite of doing that is required to live in the state of happiness. 'Being' is the need of the hour. Once you are in a state of happiness, everything else from success, tranquillity, peace and abundance will follow. So, how does one unlearn the tactical art of changing the paradigm of 'doing' all the time to learn the science of 'being'?

Can you believe that cushions showed me the way for this? Read on to know how...

The Cushions Show the Way

When we enter a meditation campus, it is with preconceived perspectives from the world that we have been living in. We have been conditioned to believe more is better — More the merrier! More thrill! More drugs! More alcohol! More space for self! More of that tasty food! More of cigarettes! More time for self! More money! Aha! This is a given and we have totally bought into the idea that money can buy happiness. No, I am not going all preachy about why one should not have more, or if the conditioning is right or wrong. This is what it is, is it not? I might be stating a fact (almost).

A bit preachy will do. The need for more, more of everything including the small things in life, is such a constant desire that it has been taken for granted and accepted, as though this is how life should be. If you don't fit the category of wanting more, you have no passion, desire and zest to live life. Don't get me wrong here. I coach people to want abundance and live a life of passion. The fun in this is when you have the desire and not be attached to it. How can one achieve this dual, almost unnatural, living? Ha! The dreaded word-attachment props up. Yes, it is to be dreaded till the time we drop it. Easier said than done, right? I got my answers as experiences as I struggled my way through the 10 days of the mental boot camp at the Vipassana centre.

So, here we were; 54 of us in total, starting the first day at the Vipassana centre in Nashik, Maharaṣhtra. Vipassana means seeing within. As you already know, you cannot use the physical eyes to see within, unless you are peering into someone else's eyes using an endoscopic microscope. To see within your own self, you will have to use the mind. You will have to turn your mind inwards and watch your own self. You might state, "Hey, I do this every day when I see myself in the mirror, or when I see myself through others' eyes." You are right! However, you use your physical sense of eyesight to see this. Here at the camp, you are taught to become aware of the power of your mind and its faculty of focus to lead you on a journey, which only you can go. By the time my 10 days at the camp were over, I had gone through loving the experience to absolutely dreading it at times.

When was the last time you used your mind for really heavy lifting? Ask yourself when was the last time you used your mind to its full potential. When was the last time you were aware that you have a mind with immense potential to do some really great work? The fun part is, even if you have never used your mind for a long time, this boot camp will give you enough exercise for it to be actively engaged with living a full life … provided you follow through and do as the technique stipulates. More about the technique later.

You must have noticed, or not, that I have prepared a nice little backdrop of the "more concept." Keep that in mind and picture these 54 people entering the large meditation hall — the size of the hall varies depending on where you will be going through the camp. The first thing you notice as you enter is that you have been deprived of the thrill of choosing your own places. Alas! The management has earmarked a place for you. Uh oh! Yours is right next to a window and you conjure all the things that can be wrong with that choice and how you could have chosen a better place not so far from the front row or away from where the mosquitoes can enter and have a field day sucking the life out of you. And hey, wait... what about my sitting cushion and the pillow I have been provided with? It looks so tiny. Is it even enough? Oh no, I am not going to wait to experiment! I know I need more pillows to support my bum, even though you have no clue you already want more. By the time it took to register all this, I realise that the much-faster, smarter minds have already picked up a couple or more of the pillows from the back of the hall and walked up to their seating places. I was left standing there with a look of utter bewilderment and shock. How could I even take so long just to register the scene and I was left with the last of the lot and they were not even good enough! I console myself that they all might be aware exactly how comfortable they were with more pillows and that was why they acted as they did. Not to give you a hard time, but just so that they have a good time. You really want to believe at this time that no one intends to cause grief to others, but they are just looking out for themselves and want to be comfortable. No, don't discard the pillows as inconsequential, yet. The lesson that emerges from these very pillows is interesting, to say the least. The lesson emerges over the next 3–4 days. And when I saw the insight the pillows brought, you quietly thanked myself for not rushing into the idea that I needed more.

Now, here is the process...

So you start getting pally with the spot you are allowed, you make peace with it and you get the pillows to mould themselves to your size and shape. The initial one hour or so passes with relative ease and you start the process of getting anchored in the present moment. You have now begun to focus on your breathing. You have been instructed clearly, articulately, and with words that are chosen to make the maximum impact to focus on respiration — Just your natural respiration. This step leads to action #1 of 2, which are the key two actions that you will carry when you fly home. It leads to becoming aware of the present moment. Your focus on natural respiration draws your mind's attention from all its wandering to only one laser-like focus. Focus on the respiration and narrow it down further to feel the flow of air on the triangular area of the nose where the air moves.

As you are giving it your best shot to focus, you hear sounds of moving pillows and ruffling of fabric and all sorts of movements behind you, beside you and all over. The concept of more has started to fire back. As your eyes are closed, you can only hear and imagine what is going on. While this imagination is shaping up, the greater truth hits home — you have lost your attention from breathing to that of your sense of hearing. Along with this sense kicking in, because you don't open your eyes, you also start feeling that the body has started manifesting the absolute discomfort it is going through. The mind is now all over the place. Somehow, you get through to the end of that first session; and boy, do you want to stretch your legs! The process has just begun. What is this process?

The closest analogy to the process that I can come up with is reprogramming. Here, the mind is being reprogrammed. New programs are being installed in the mind. Here, the old programs are not first deleted before the new ones are installed. Actually, the old ones get overwritten. This will emerge as we move through the next 10 days. You also see patterns that you never knew existed within you; that is, old programs that have been silently running in the background, taking away your precious energy and contributing misery and suffering instead of a richer, fuller life. Who would want to be running these programs? As an android generation person, you will understand that unless you actually swish off the unwanted apps running in the background, they will keep running in the background without your knowing. Also then, there are unnecessary, unwanted apps like past hurt, jealousy, hatred, grudges, greed, craving, and aversion running in the background of your mind at all times.

You can also liken the beliefs holding you back to the anchor of a ship, not allowing you to make any forward movement. An anchor being such a small piece of instrument and much lighter than the ship, can hold steady something much heavier than itself by digging into the seabed. Your cravings, aversions and other tendencies running in the background are like the anchors that dig deep into the seabed of your mind and are now holding you back. The only movement that can occur is going around in circles like a ship does from the point where the anchor has taken root.

Who would want to be stuck? Who would want to have some unknown apps ruining their battery power and not allowing the complete use of their potential? Who would not want to sail the oceans and see the world? Who would not want to experience life fully living the purpose that life has designed. Continuing on the analogy of the ship, which is also called a vessel at times. You are like that magnificent ship with the best technology to make you sail powerfully across the seven seas. Call into ports that offer some great experiences. However, you have decided to stay stuck to one place and not use any of your systems, engine or technology to move ahead. And when you want to move you realise there is no captain for your ship. Without the captain being present and yet having a whole crew ready for your disposal there can only be chaos, even if you have managed to heave anchor and move. The captain of your ship is your mindfulness; it's the ability of the mind to be aware. The captain can chart a course, help you to heave your anchors and start the process of moving ahead, gather speed and go full steam ahead towards the destination plotted out. He helps you get into safe harbours and protects the vessel from storms and squalls. Who would want to have a weak captain for their ship? Who would want a captain who is engaged in activities that are ineffective and unproductive? Would you want a captain that sabotages his own ship? If you want to have a strong captain then you got to provide the right tools, techniques, knowledge and training. You begin by first identifying the present status and then reprogram to suit the requirements of having a powerful, well-built, wise and centred captain.

This reprogramming occurs throughout the day at the time slots mentioned; at times it is done in group sittings, and at times, isolated by the self in a 4x6 feet cell. This is your conscious effort. Now, because you are taking action your mind continues the job even when you go to sleep. It's as though you have started a download by clicking the download button and left it running; every now and then you see that the download is in progress and it shows you that there is movement.

The sessions are as follows:

04.30 – 06.30

08.00 – 09.00

09.00 – 11.00

13.00 – 14.30

14.30 – 17.00

18.00 – 19.00

19.00 – 20.30

20.30 – 21.00

Approximately 9 to 9-and-a-half hours each day will be sitting time over the next ten days. You don't go that far as to think of day 10. You don't want to go there. This being my second time I could see how I went through my first 10-day course at Penang. I went there with an all too common, typical achiever's mentality — I will not quit the course in-between and come back. I will go through the 10 days. I might have focused more energy and power living this desire that I missed out on some valuable inputs which I received during my second 10-day course, well, this was my lesson and I had to learn it that way; there is no good or bad, right or wrong way.

By now you must have noticed that all the observations, thoughts, and patterns are occurring in the mind. In my mind, and as you have been reading here, have been thought forms that have been triggered off as an effect to your reading. And who was it that was actually doing the reading?

Oh no, no… I am not trying to get you into a knot here by asking the age-old, almost-unanswerable question — WHO AM I? I am putting you on the spot to observe, to notice, to pay attention, to focus on what has been happening as you have been reading. Where did the reading happen? Who read it? Was there any reaction? Where was the reaction? Did it show as any physical action too? If you don't convince me otherwise, I'll have to let you settle for knowing that it was your mind that was doing all of the above. Your eyes were only a portal for receiving information. Your hands were holding the book and played only the part of supporting the mind. If you happened to hear the book, then your ears only helped you to receive the information. So okay, you don't agree that the mind is everything, then take Gotama Buddha's simplest of statements and work with it — "The Mind precedes all phenomenon."

Now, I am not enlightened, nor am I taking you purely on a spiritual journey; or else at this point in time I would have introduced the mind-bending variable of consciousness for the purpose of this book. It is a good start to agree that we are dealing with the mind and believing that it is the source from which life happens. I would go to the extent of stating that our senses too are part of the mind; they are in the mind.

Do take note: The mind is not restricted to the brain. Mind can be in the brain as much as it can be in your toe or anywhere else. It really is everywhere and in everything, and also, everywhere and everything is in the mind. Don't fall off the grid and stop reading at this point in time; It's only here that the math is difficult, the rest of the book is just a breeze; and what is more, if you take appropriate action on reading this book and start your own self-happiness project, it will not be long before you make your own breakthrough discoveries and realise it experientially that mind is all there is, really. The rest are just the props for this grand movie to keep running.

So we have tepidly established that we will play along the lines that the mind is all. If the mind is all, then it is super critical for us to understand its working and harness its powers. How much of your mind's power are you using right now? Well, you could take all the IQ tests and stuff and come up with fancy numbers topping the charts. That is only one facet of the mind — the intellect.

What about your happiness? What about your habits? What about your relationships? How about wealth and abundance? Are you living life's purpose intended for you? Are you in control of the mind or is your mind controlling you?

You might ask me that if it is the mind that is in control, how can you ever be in control of it? Well, that's where the fun part is. You are really blessed or cursed, depending on the way you look at it. Life has thrown you this opportunity with ample skills. The fact that you are reading this book is proof enough that you are blessed, because (a) you are still alive! Is that good or what!? (b) that means you have eyes (c) you are able to read so I assume you have some sort of education (d) Also, so far you have been able to make some sense of the ideas I have presented here, which means you have the faculty of your mind working for you and you are in control, yes?

Let's plough on. You do have the ability to control your mind. Whether you are tapping into this ability to live your life is a question only you will be able to answer. Even if you are not tapping into it, know that you can. The science of how the mind works is explained in detail in many books and you might want to take a dip into that ocean of knowledge to learn more. The premise of this book is not to delve deeper into the functioning of the mind but to start at a point where we know and understand that it is a powerful tool; it has numerous programs which are running. These programs make us do what we do. As you saw, the entire play of events, thoughts and actions for the 54 participants was unique in a way and we all acted based on our existing programming and habit patterns in the mind.

What happened over the next 3 days was that new programs got installed. In doing so, some of the old programs were overwritten. You might be wondering how a simple act of just sitting for 9-and-half hours a day for 3 days could install new programs in one's mind. The new programs are your new habits. And yes, you can form new habits at any point in time of your life. Want to know how?

Mind and its Malleability

New habits can be created

Can you hold a gun and fire it too?

Can you run 10 kms every Sunday starting from the first Sunday after reading this book?

Can you only run wherever you go from now on?

Can you eat your meals in 3 minutes from the time they are served?

Can you sleep for 4 hours only and yet work at optimum efficiency?

Well, if you thought you cannot do all or many of these now, guess what, I could not do any of these too before I joined the Indian Navy. In a matter of 2 months I was able to do all of the above. Not only do these but consistently continue doing so for the next 4 months too, some of them for the next couple of years until I decided I did not want to keep up with some of them. Talk about eating in 3 minutes! Who would want to continue this? If I so wanted I could keep doing them. These were new habits that I had formed, none of these existed before I joined the Navy.

This shows that habits make it possible to live our lives; it is imperative that our habits are aligned to our purpose. If your purpose and habits are not aligned, try as you might, but you will not be able to see the result. For instance, if your purpose is to lose weight, and let's say your present habits include sleeping late, not exercising, eating food without being aware of the nutrition or the ill effects of the food, it's a no-brainer that if you continue living your habits you will not be getting any closer to your goals or purpose. It pays to have habits in line with what you want life to give you.

Dr. Goenka's art of creating new mind patterns using repetition is effective and lasting. During the 10 day Vipassana, course Dr. Goenka uses his gift wisely and for the benefit of each student. Every hour, when you start the practice, the complete set of instructions is repeated with clear, and precise words and chants. It was like teaching a child to write. First you draw a dotted line image of a letter. You instruct the child. You now see that dotted line, use your pencil to write on it, write it a few times till it gets to darker shades of the pencil or chalk or whatever it is that suits your teaching method. The mind gets imprinted with this writing from outside in. After repeated practice, the next time you tell the child to write that particular letter verbally, the mind will reproduce it through the hand.

This is what happened to most of us during the course. Hour after hour, the dotted line was made to be written on, darken it, and deepen it. The mind, being malleable and fluid, gets the deep neural pathways to follow the instructions even in a deep sleep. This makes you aware that your conscious mind is just the tip of the iceberg. There is a deeper part of your mind which is huge, powerful and constantly aware. Would you like IT to be your friend to navigate you through this life or you would want it to be subdued by your limited conscious mind, which is awake only during your waking period and shuts off when you sleep? The process of tapping into the malleable features of the mind begin with the awareness of the breath; and ever so slowly, you start seeing the effects ... Moment by moment

The day begins with rigorous work on day 1 itself. Most, if not all, are not used to a 4 am wake up call. Even as you manage to drag yourself to the meditation hall or to your 4 feet by 6 feet cell, you are half awake, half asleep. Maybe that works to your advantage too as you can't really fall asleep sitting in a lotus position for the next two hours.

Unknown to you yet, there is a pattern emerging in the seating pillows. If you look closely you will find the once-fluffy pillows are now moulding themselves to receive the weight, shape and contours of the person using them. In my instance, it was mine, of course, and not someone else's. They were forming into something new, something different. I also realised that the pillows were being folded, twisted, made into smaller sizes using the ingenuity of who was using them. I just observed this with no connections made yet.

I did not know it yet on the first day, nor had I seen the pattern emerge. It was only towards the end of the 4th or 5th day that I made a connection between the flexibility and malleability of the cushions and the changes in my mind.

As you sit through the hour-after-hour of meditation, there are a few significant actions that are occurring due to your mindfulness:

(A) You have started observing your respiration — natural, normal breathing — no calisthenics or dramatic breathing. One of the highlights of this course for me has always been the simplicity of the actions. There is no requirement to change a thing in the way you are. You are a hard breather. That goes, you are in. Oh, you breathe slow and steady; so what, that is fine too! Well, you take deep breaths? Be my guest! You don't fit into any of the breathing categories I just described? Guess what, it's OK!

(B) You are sitting down in one place — When was the last time you sat in one place, in one position, for more than an hour and was actually aware of your every breath, your every move? Good on you! You remember! I could not, because the most I was practicing was a 45-minute stretch a day for a year before my second course

(C) You are following the rules of the camp and living by the code of conduct prescribed. — This is a good time to introduce the three codes that you will be following:

The foundation of the practice is **Sīla.** Moral conduct.

Sīla provides a basis for the development of **Samādhi.** This is the concentration and purification of the mind, which is achieved through **Paññā**, the wisdom of insight.

These small, mindful actions don't seem like much on the surface yet; however, they have already started a chain reaction within your so-called sub0conscious mind. I could not resist using this analogy; the most common one used for the subconscious mind is the way Freud described it. Think of an iceberg. Now picture the tip of the iceberg. That tip is your conscious mind. The big, humungous part of the iceberg which is submerged is your subconscious mind. I don't have to say this, but the depth of the submerged part of the iceberg is vast in comparison to the tip. Guess what though! We use a part of the conscious mind and think we are on top of the world. Imagine what you could do if you had the knowhow and access to that deep mind?

So, your simple, mindful actions have triggered an avalanche. As yet, there is no physical manifestation other than the pain that you have started feeling. You are squirming, adjusting, changing postures and doing a lot to manage the pain. There is one process which you cannot miss though. You start by being present. Present where? You are in the sacred presence of the most powerful catalyst — THE NOW. Nothing fancy, right? You are always in the NOW! You cannot be anywhere else but here and now. The only flipside is that you don't know this. The profoundness of this simple, mindful action is that you are now aware that you are in the present moment. You have started developing your mind's awareness of the present moment.

For me, just this one action; just one action if taken consistently, moment by moment, is liberation indeed. The mind instantly gets access to such vast free space that it opens up infinite possibilities of how you could live life. Don't go yet! There is so much more to this. Like that say in Bollywood movies, "*picture abhi baki hai*!"

Let's fast-forward to the pattern that becomes visible over the next 5 days. The mind has adopted itself to the sequence and created new habit patterns; and irrespective of the number of pillows used to sit on, it has flexibly turned into plastic to a comfortable position, and no matter if you have 1 or 5 cushions, the mind has adjusted and created new pathways to sit for long hours in the position you had chosen and honed over the last 50 hours or so. It goes to prove that the mind is so flexible and malleable that within a short span of time, by being in the presence of the only truth that there is — 'The Now'. By diligent, constant attention to this moment, new habit patterns have been formed. The new patterns were not kept for a later time by procrastinating on the excuse of breaking old patterns. New patterns were recorded, and in response, the old patterns dissolved. It was by observing the cushions take shape to our sitting positions that I was led by the hand, so to say, to see the elasticity of the mind.

The pain of the body had reduced considerably and now the mind was comfortable. The mind-body interaction was just fantastic. Here was a classic example. What I learnt was that a new habit was created over a span of just 6–7 days. The new habit overwrote the old one. In this instance, the old habit was to sit on a chair. Every time the concept of sitting came to mind it was to sit on a chair. Instead of breaking that habit of sitting on a chair, it was simply replaced by sitting down over long hours. So, new habits are easier to create than to stop, break or even give up old habits.

It's easy, right? There is one catch. Resistance. Resistance from the belief systems that run your life. Steven Pressfield nails it in his book, *The War of Art*. "Rule of thumb: the more important a call to action is to our soul's evolution, the more resistance we will feel toward pursuing it."

In this case, if your call to action is to start a new habit as simple as waking up in the morning, to sit quietly, etc., you will face resistance in the form of your belief systems. Let's see how the beliefs rule.

The Cell - #11

Being an old student — old, not as in age; you could be 18 and yet be called an old student; 'Old fella' if you have previously attended a 10-day course. So, by these standards I was an old student. Old students get nudged towards the deep end of the pool so that you can get better at the technique.

I remember my swimming lessons in the pool and how my friends taught me when I was 6 or 7 years. It was totally wild. For a week they allowed me to use a floater around my waist in chest-high water; but once in a while, pushing me in without the floater after having explained the technique and also having demonstrated it. The second week, as I was just beginning to enjoy the water and make it a short distance in the shallow end, I was literally dragged and thrown into the deep end; you flounder as though you have just lost your life already. I came up to take a breath and the lessons I was taught kicked in. I made my longest two or three stroke length towards the poolside. The feeling when I made it to the edge alive was nothing short of a miracle. A similar miracle occurs when you get into the depth of yourself. You learn to survive, thrive even.

In this instance, in a way, you are nudged forward, so to say, towards going a bit deeper within yourself. So it was over the 10 days: I spent around 60 hours of the total 120 hours, in total, in a cell just 6 feet long and 4 feet wide. It was rigorous and hard work like the two-three stroke length which took me forever to cover. Not because of the physical discomfort that I had felt more profoundly. It was because the operation into the deeper areas of the mind picked up intensity. When this starts — old, really old stuff gets hit afresh. You are left mesmerised one instance and in severe misery the next. It's like you are shown a mirror and there are no filters when you look at it. It is just the raw truth of what has occurred.

This cell is a paradox. It does not confine you. On the contrary, it liberates you from the deepest bondages of your mind. It purifies you. You might not be able to relate to this process with intellect alone. This was a cell of liberation. The experience that I share is only a reference point. You will have to try it out for getting your own experience. Well, this was not a cell like what you would think, although it helps people in those types of cells too.

This being my second experience, I had a bit more maturity than my first experience. The 300-plus hours of meditation since my last year's meditation and introduction to this technique have been the reason for the awareness and maturity I brought to my time in the cell. This cell represents the belief systems that we have built in, around, and within ourselves. We have confined ourselves to these beliefs.

Read the next chapter and notice if you get challenged with this new set of assumptions I am trying to create. If you find it obnoxious, absurd and stupid, then you will know how the mind has latched on to only one pattern of thinking, which it has bought into to be right.

A New Belief to an Old Equation $E=MC^2$

Hey, so what about the belief in enlightenment and how we have looked at it so far? What if our existing theory and beliefs get challenged and you are asked to consider something like what Einstein actually showed us — that $E=mc^2$ is for enlightenment? Here goes a mind-bending belief on what Einstein wanted to explain.

Enlightenment = Mindfulness x Consciousness (squared)

Enlightenment! The word itself is like the holy grail. The moment I use the word, I am sure some of you will not even bother to read further because they have labelled enlightenment as only for the mystics and spiritual people. After labelling, the people are put in a box. Often, those in this box are called "abnormal" by the so-called normal people. The common misunderstanding is that ordinary people don't have enlightenment. Sometimes, there is even fear to use the word among your close circle of friends because then they put you in a box called 'sadhu', 'baba', or 'guru'. It is quiet hilarious at times to come across such situations.

On putting people in boxes, here is what transpired recently — I was with two kindred souls, sitting and having a nice hot cup of coffee. Both are exceptionally well off in their respective areas of expertise. One is a trendsetter in the field of training/coaching and the other is a marketing and sales genius. Now, the coach uses his unique style of coaching people to come out of their limiting beliefs. His style is unconventional. However, the human mind sees the uniqueness and starts to relatively compare it with other well-known personalities. They put that person in a box, saying, "you are like a Dr. Demartini" or "you are like a Richard Bandler." So much for relativity and the inherent desire to label people. Nothing wrong in pegging you with some great names. Now imagine the reverse of that — people usually downgrade and compare the other with their selves and feel better at the cost of discounting the worth of the other person. I wondered to myself why each person couldn't be appreciated for what they are. Simply accepting people as they are or things as it is seems like such a task. Similarly, the word enlightenment has been associated with connotations that make it impossible for everyday ordinary people to even go near it. It's the phenomenal power of our limiting beliefs that has created this.

For those who have dared to look at any limiting belief and question it, they can read on. Here are a few questions to begin with:

What does enlightenment mean to you?

Have you ever wondered why you cannot be enlightened?

What if I told you that enlightenment is our very nature; it is what we are. Would you want to take my word and explore it further?

To enlighten means to shed light on something. It is to give knowledge. It is to show light to someone. So you see, it is not such a biggie after all — you have always been imparting knowledge to someone through your work, through your love at home. You have been shedding light on how to do things better maybe or just being a guiding light to someone who needs you.

It is also all about light; and if we had to follow a few discoveries made to date, we find that we are all made of light — we are light. If we are light, then why do we find it so hard to believe it?

To get to the stage of empowering yourself to believe that you are light itself, you will have to question each statement and reference point. When you see through the false illusions created by those beliefs, you start the process of empowering yourself.

How can we use Einstein's equation to get on this journey?

Enlightenment equals mindfulness multiplied by consciousness squared.

To a small extent we have intellectually read what enlightenment means. If we use the equation $E=MC^2$, we see that it is not all that difficult. So the first step is we need to understand what is mindfulness and consciousness and we are on the way. So, here are the typically-labelled definitions of mindfulness and consciousness.

Mindfulness: A mental state achieved by focusing one's awareness on the present moment, while calmly acknowledging and accepting one's feelings, thoughts, and bodily sensations, used as a therapeutic technique.

Consciousness : It is the state or quality of awareness, or, of being aware of an external object or something within oneself. It has been defined as sentience, awareness, subjectivity, the ability to experience or to feel wakefulness, having a sense of selfhood.

From this statement of Max Plank, theoretical physicist who originated quantum theory, which won him the Nobel Prize in Physics in 1918, it is obvious that consciousness is very important — "I regard consciousness as fundamental. I regard matter as derivative from consciousness. We cannot get behind consciousness. Everything that we talk about, everything that we regard as existing, postulates consciousness."

Therefore, the starting point is to acknowledge that we are all enlightened beings. It is a matter of understanding how we can live as what we really are. If you can use a high quality of consciousness/awareness (square it to be sure) and focus it (be mindful) of the present moment, you have an excellent formula for enlightenment.

So, what are you waiting for? You can now experiment with mindfulness to see the result your consciousness has on matter.

Your mind creates your reality. Use it wisely!

Once your start becoming mindful, you will notice that your old belief systems will come to light and this coming to light is a liberating act.

On Bondage & Beliefs

Examine your beliefs. Are they limiting you?

I had just arrived in India and moved into a house comfortably located in a green, light, airy area aptly named "the oxygen zone." I was full of gratitude for life having provided me with this amazing break from the hard work I had put in over the last 15 years; first being a part of the Indian Navy and then travelling often as part of an oil and gas company.

Having settled in, I started with my yoga classes, was eating right and losing the excess fat I had accumulated over the last so many years of unaware eating and drinking. I was feeling really high as I was overcoming a lot of beliefs I had formed about my body, my eating habits and other activities. All was going hunky dory until one fine day I was riding the lift down from my apartment at the peak of my health and one tiny thought occurred — "Harry, this can't be happening; how could this peak health be yours to have? This is not how it is supposed to be." Now I had read a bit to understand that my upper limiting belief system was kicking in and observed the thought pass by without holding on to it.

I should have continued on the upward spiral isn't it? Guess what, I picked up the flu the next day, a round of antibiotics and the path of recovery to health again.

It took me a month to get back up and recommence my yoga sessions. All ordinary living, right? We all pick up the flu and stuff, but the chances are we never pause to think of when these events occur. Going forward you might want to observe the moments where you tend to slide down. Were you riding high up one moment and then — out of nowhere — boom! You are sliding downwards with a fierce speed that has the potential to take you all the way down.

What had happened? I am not used to having peak performing health because of my fear of a childhood conditioning where every time I got on to something that I loved, say, like the time I got selected for the hockey team and I fell sick and bed-ridden for a week. And because this happened so many times, I had created a belief system around peak health. I could never have it. So I stayed on the sidelines, not doing what I loved or not taking any chances, thinking that if I don't do anything outrageous or adventurous I will fall sick. This worked for a while, but then there came a time when I had to break free of this belief and take flight. I could not live a life on the sidelines. I took risks, challenged my beliefs and grew into peak health and did not look back, especially through my years in the Indian Navy. It took me by surprise that the old program was still lurking somewhere in the background, and given enough attention, it could strengthen itself to be manifested as matter.

Have you experienced this?

Maybe not with health, but with other areas of life. What about wealth? Relationships? Jobs?

Going back to my meditation cell where I spent hours a day. Our limiting beliefs are the walls of the cell that we have created — we want to stay inside because we cannot handle the scene outside of those walls. My time in the cell brought to light the many instances I had literally orchestrated my own slide downwards. I also realised that unknown, unresolved issues buried deep down as bound vibrations move upwards and outwards on the physical realm of the body. My body started developing rashes; I felt my tongue start to brush against ulcers inside my mouth. I was not doing anything that warranted these rashes. Just sitting quietly, the silence was only on the outside; meanwhile, on the inside, the mental voice continued to rise in pitch and volume. Just being aware that there is the presence of a mental voice, and watching it closely with a laser-like focus starts a process of healing. The impurities rise to the surface and are dispelled. The bound, tightly-wound knots in your vibrations loosen up and unravel. As they dissipate, they leave behind scars of healing.

I became aware that I if toyed with what was coming up, it was a loop of no return. I understood the concept of relaxing into the sensations that were being thrown up and releasing them. I began to relax physically too, deeper and deeper; and as more of the old stuff surfaced, the more I relaxed, thus being able to release more. After each of the two-hour sessions that I walked out of the cell, there was a feeling of lightness; a smile playing around the edge. Oh yes, there were also moments of absolute sadness overwhelming me when I walked out of there.

The vibrations elevate to higher frequencies as you release the old patterns that had formed deep within the mind. The sensations of the body keep indicating your journey. Meditating from moment to moment, living life from the wisdom of experiencing 'the release' when you don't judge or react impulsively is what creates new possibilities. You start opening a door to new possibilities when you spend time working on yourself without wanting to change or be in control of the result.

Just by being present in this moment and focusing your breathing, realising you have come this far. What more can there be to experience?

The next section brings to light how our reactions from the stored memory of the mind and the karmic cycle mire us deep into a mental loop of suffering. If you have to harness the power of your presence, which harnesses the power of now, you will have to observe every moment so mindfully that you become aware of the reactions that arise from every life situation you are experiencing at that moment.

Before you jump to the next section you might want to check your present state and the speed bumps that you have laid down.

Are you a Bond or Bound?

Simple steps to begin your enquiry into the limiting beliefs that might be stopping you from being the best version of you.

1. Notice how conscious you are of the thoughts passing through you mind. Notice that sometimes, even you are not doing anything, your consciousness or awareness is just floating around without focusing on anything.
2. Now, focus your awareness to observe the present moment. Observe the sensations occurring in your body (you can go for a Vipassana course to practice this technique). Observe your breathing; observe every action you are taking. If you are walking, observe how it feels.
3. Spend some time everyday being aware with your mind and experience living an enlightened life.

The by-products of being acutely aware of the present moment are:

- Wisdom of our own ignorance
- Insights about our limiting beliefs
- Tremendous amounts of unlimited energy

- Abundance of love and light in every major area of your life
- Most importantly, you will not get swayed by the highs and lows of life situations. You will be in harmony with life itself.

Now, list all the beliefs that limit you; some guidance in the form of question below. Write down a reason why for any answer that you choose.

1. I can achieve anything I can put my mind to. YES/NO
2. I am a creator and not just at the mercy of circumstances, people and life. YES/NO
3. I have set a limit to the abundance I can have because there's only so much I can handle. YES/NO
4. I have set a limit to the best health I can have because I cannot see myself having anything better than that. YES/NO
5. I can have the best of relationships in life. YES/NO

Now read through your answers as you begin taking baby steps to uncover the hidden beliefs that have kept you from achieving some of your dreams. Take time to examine the line of abundance you have drawn beyond which you cannot go. This could be because someone in your childhood and school kept telling you that you cannot do anything beyond this!

What about your health? Have you been told that

you would remain fat and inflexible ... and have you believed them or even your own self tell you that? Now, take the time to question that belief.

Have you seen yourself attract relationships that never allow you to grow in life? Are your relationships with people tiring, unhelpful and highly corrosive? Who is attracting these relationships?

This is your journey into self-awareness. There are no answers or solutions that I can tell you. Your innate wisdom will take over as you get more familiar with your inner limits and see or even hear your limits drive your behaviour and attitude. When you see that the personality that you have formed is restricted in many ways just by your own thinking, you will also find doors opening within that will lead you to explore your unlimited potential and get you on the frequency that makes things manifest as fast as thought can travel.

SECTION 2

IT'S NOT FOREVER ANYWAYS

Being Level-Headed

"NOTHING REAL CAN BE THREATENED. NOTHING UNREAL EXISTS…"

– A Course in Miracles

Have you heard the phrase, "he is a level-headed person"; you must have, if you have not, then at least you have now. Now, when you hear or read of this phrase, whose mind pops into your head? Maybe you are that person. For a long time I thought the head was the seat of all power. I also attributed my relative successes and failures to my head. I remember commenting at times, "I can't get my head around this problem," and other times have I heard myself say, "My head hurts with all this thinking."

As I continue on the path of knowing myself a little more with each moment, I am led to doors that open to some amazing wisdom. One such door opened my perception to see it was not the head that was not getting around the problem, nor was it the head that was doing the thinking. It was the mind. I also experienced that this 'mind' was an independent being. At that time it seemed to be out of any control. There are many instances, even now, where it behaves like a jerk. Well, who can control the mind? A question for another time, I reckon.

What is important to know now is that the mind is all. It is not easy to fathom this, forget not easy — it is really difficult to get this principle and experience it too. The mind is the source and this is what it is. To get around it, ask yourself the following questions

1. When was the last time you did something in which the first impulse did not come from a thought? You might say I brushed my teeth without even thinking about it. Really?

   Come up with anything and go back to the start of it. You will find that it always leads to you having a thought first. You think and act.

2. Who had that thought? Can your body have a thought?
3. Did the thought become an action?
4. Did that action lead to creating some result? In the instance of brushing teeth, it led you to have cleaner teeth.

So, what we see is that thoughts are the first form of energy that the mind creates and this leads to creating of matter or action as a physically manifested form.

Now, let's take a scenario. You are watching a movie. I know the movie analogy is so old and used so extensively you will instinctively run down to the end of this paragraph — but no, hang on! This is a funny one!

Which is the movie that you have really been influenced by? Let it be. Now, picture yourself watching that movie; for the sake of this book we will consider a movie by one of the superstars of India, say its Shah Rukh khan. He has the ability to make the audience watching his movies in a movie hall laugh, cry, fear, hate and a volley of intense emotions. During one such emotional scene where he has been shot and is almost dying, you too are there in the movie hall. When you see that particular scene, your mind activates the necessary emotional response. However, you soon a hold over yourself and look around to realise that this was just a movie scene and also occur to you that the movie star might be having a good time elsewhere. You choose not to react. As you watch the movie unfold; and it being a movie, you see that the actor's life gets miraculously saved by a small bullet-proof metal plate, which was right where the bullet hits him. In this situation, there are viewers who get so emotionally invested in the scene that there was once the case of a viewer, who, taken up by the intense emotions, got up from his seat and ran towards the screen with a pocket knife, throwing it at the movie star onscreen, shouting, "Save yourself, man! You have it in you!" Of course, a dramatic reaction that led to embarrassment and amused reactions from all around!

Who in this scene is level-headed?

Now, you can laugh your butt off and dismiss this as a joke. However, if you stay just a bit longer, you will relate to this situation in a practical way. How many times have you lost your cool, shouted, thrown a tantrum, suppressed anger, sadness and fear all because of something happening on the screen and you got emotionally invested in it as a reality? Have you been level-headed? Have you taken a moment to take a breath, look around, see and realise that it was just a movie. Or are you the person who takes the movie seriously enough to run over to help the projected images thrown on the screen by the play of light and sound?

In any case, there is a movie playing — one that is playing on the screen called your mind. It can get very real. As you observed, whatever you can think of can be manifested into matter. So, you have the power to make your thoughts come alive. Also, you can cause damage to yourself and others by getting involved in the play of light and sound. Being level-headed gives you that moment of clarity, the ability to take a deep breath and call a spade a spade and not attach an emotional charge and its associated reaction. Better still, the moment passes on and you are moving on to the next moment.

Being level-headed calls for observing the situation, event or form unfolding in that moment for what it is and taking a moment before reacting to it. Here is where the two dots get connected. Learning to become vigilant and focusing the mind only on that moment is where you become aware of the passing impermanence of those situations.

If everything is impermanent, then why have violent reactions to it?

Reactions

The Art of Making Stock

Here is an analogy I can use: A few months ago, I signed up for an online cooking course; and one of the recipes I learned and practiced was making vegetarian and non-vegetarian stock (soup) for storing over longer periods of time and having it handy for making soups and other dishes. You take the raw vegetables or any of the meat you wish to prepare the stock from, cut it into pieces; wash it thoroughly to ensure it is clean; add just enough water to submerge the ingredients you have taken in the cooking pot. The mixture at this point is clean and clear. Now, place the pot over a stove squarely and start up the heat. Keep the heat just enough to simmer the stock and not to boil. Over the next few hours (4–5 hours) of simmering, seemingly clear water which you started with, turns a different shade, and also, there are impurities surfacing slowly which you never knew existed in the mixture or were able to see at the beginning. As the impurities surface, you take the impurities off the mixture with the ladle. After multiple passes of clearing the surface impurities, the stock starts getting cleaner. As the hours trickle, by you see the stock getting ready to be cooled and preserved to form part of a tasty meal as and when required. A very integral and important action here is not to interfere with the process, not to stir or agitate the mixture, and to have just enough heat to avoid boiling over.

With Vipassana, this happens to our mind and body. No, no, don't run away yet! You are not cut into parts and cooked over the fire — not physically at least — but in a way, you can relate to it. You already are a mixture of many ingredients, the major ones being your body and mind. So you might see yourself as a clear mixture at the beginning of the process. What you do know are the times when you are miserable and suffered because of these miseries. So when you start the process of purification of the mind and body, you sit squarely, and as comfortably on a cushion and a pillow — like the pot is made to sit on the stove. The low heat in this instance is the focus of your mind. You are trained to develop this intense focus with a proven technique which has been practiced and honed over the last 2,500 years. Miracles occur as you sit and pay focused attention over the many hours of meditation for day with just enough break time so that you don't break.

What happens is something similar to the impurities that bubble up to the surface of the stock mixture. Your deep-rooted impurities start surfacing. These impurities manifest themselves as gross sensations — pain, or at times, subtle sensations on the body — as you continue to sit and watch without interfering with the process. Without agitation or boiling, without creating likes or dislikes to the various sensations manifesting on the surface of your body, the deep-rooted, once-unseen impurities start to dissolve and get eliminated. And you too are left with a clear, clean state of presence. In this state there is only love, compassion and kindness. The after-effects of this cleansing process leave you with qualities, capabilities and abilities which are beneficial not only to you but to everyone you come in contact with.

An interesting insight that came out was that when you prepare a non-vegetarian stock the impurities that surface are more and take longer to eliminate. On the other hand, a vegetarian stock has lesser and lighter impurities. So, the message was very clear to me. If you keep putting meat in your food, you will keep having to spend longer working on your body and mind to purify. So, one of the changes I am implementing is moving towards a predominantly vegetarian diet.

Some of the other benefits which get thrown in are:

1. You learn that it is difficult to break old habits, but you can create new habit patterns that overwrite the old ones. For instance, instead of struggling with giving up the habit of smoking, you create a new habit pattern. The new pattern could be as simple as breathing deeply when the craving to smoke arises. The craving goes away. The technique sharpens your mind to become aware of your sensation to crave and activates a non-reactive response.

2. You become aware of the importance of living an aware life — aware of the present moment. You learn through experience that each moment, sensation and thought are impermanent and this, in turn, starts dimming your attachment to the future and its imagined consequences. You end up liberating the craving within, you start living a simpler, happier life.
3. You start using the power of focusing the mind to achieve results at work which are not only better but faster. You realise you can do the same amount of work in less time than before without feeling hurried or stressed about it.
4. Your health starts to improve. The innate wisdom within the body, along with the mindful awareness that you develop, hastens you towards creating many healthy lifestyle changes.

This meditation technique is a scientific experiment you should undertake at least once in your lifetime. No words of mine can express the urgency and compassion with which I would like you to get to the first course available in your vicinity. Treat this as a lean start-up business model, i.e., check and verify as soon as you can if this is working, and if not, make a pivot in your strategy. To get to the pivot point you need to first experience and gather feedback. So, just do it. Go for it!

A few of the many good aspects of this is — It is non-religions, free of cost, you do not have to chant or be part of any arcane rite or ritual, and neither will it challenge your present God or religious sentiments.

Now that you have dissolved the impurities and started getting cozy with a new and liberating mindset, what next? It's like the cup has been emptied; don't you want to fill it up again? If you answered affirmatively to that, let's look at what new possibilities you could be in for.

Are you LIGHT Enough?

Sitting through one of the evening discourses of Dr Goenka, I was listening to him, but at the same time, there seemed to be a thought wanting to register itself within me — I was reminded of my son. I worked from home and usually got engrossed in something I was writing or doing. He came into the room and stood there quietly for a few seconds. Of course, I sensed his presence and I was also aware that he knew that dad was working and should not be disturbed. Less than a minute after he came in, he said, "Can I say something, Dad?" He made it sound as though it was very important; I could not say No. So, I told him to go ahead; at this time I had to focus on him completely. Now, sometimes, he has profound things to say and show me and at times it is something which could have waited and could have passed away without a second thought even if he had not asked. For example, there have been times when he has come in and showed me his new Lego masterpiece that he created; he shares the story behind the masterpiece and how it will be something for the new earth when it arrives and this machine will help people navigate in the new earth. This concept of a new earth coming from him is always fascinating. Other times, he just say, "Dad, you know, I drank water and feel good now."

Similarly, when I was watch the discourse I was totally engrossed and this thought waited, albeit impatiently, to say something. And as it happens with my son, some of it is profound and some of it is just a passing cloud. At this point of time, I don't know if what came to me during this phase is relevant or just a fleeting thought, but then I would rather say it and leave it to you, the reader, to make a call on its relevance.

All efforts during the 10-day course is to move away from pain — Pain caused due to suffering. The effort is to eliminate misery. The way of doing it is interesting yet hard and takes up a lot of time and energy. What is happening though is that we are observing the basic element of nature as a vibration. What we are doing each minute of those 10 days and then the practice of years thereafter, if we practice, is to observe our frequency of vibration. We are not trying to actually change the frequency of our vibration or alter it or even desire a change (this is debatable, will come to it later); the paradox is, "if you consciously know you are not desiring it, does it mean you started with an innate desire in the first place?"

So, with this ongoing effort, you observe that the sensations of the body are related to the frequencies of liberation. When I was observing these gross and painful sensations, blank, blind, and heavy, I sensed I was on the heavier, deeper vibrations that took an immense amount of energy and focus. I could not even focus on any higher, subtler, lighter vibrations or sensations of the body. The sensations of the body are directly linked to the vibration of the universe. When we experience a pain from the past, it manifests in the present moment as heavy, dense and dumb sensations. Nothing to run away from. The learning that these vibrations bring is liberating.

I pictured that there are various frequencies which are in a continuous flux along a spiral shape and each frequency has a colour except the one that is right adjacent to the one I am on right now, which at that time was a sensation of aches and heaviness; and the one right next to me was going at a speed which was phenomenally fast. It was really fast. It was like multiple train tracks moving at varying speeds — and you, being at the centre of the various tracks. Now, your speed is determined by the life you are living. If you are experiencing pain, misery, jealousy, hatred etc., then you are on a particular speed. To get to the one right next to you, which for me is the frequency of light, is that you really need to accelerate to match the speed of that frequency. This acceleration of the speed, unlike the speeding you do in your car or other vehicles, is actually achieved by slowing down.

The more you slow down, the higher your light-speed will seem to get. Sounds counter-intuitive only till the time you experience it. How can you experience it? Simply by observing your present vibration. I don't know how, nor do I have scientific data or formulae to prove this, but I know through experience that as you slow down and observe each breath, as you slow down and observe each sensation, as you train your mind to focus sharply, you are getting closer to the speed of light and there come these tiny moments... milliseconds... when you enter a gap where you actually have got on to the running train of light; and then get back to a different, yet present, reality.

This gap IS Step 101. As you speed up enough by slowing down, your awareness of the present moment gets better and you keep getting into that space more often. This slowing manifests as your gross, painful, blank, and blind sensations of the body turn to subtle sensations. I have not reached any state of dissolution, so lack the experience of it; however, the lighter you get, the more you move towards the experience of dissolution.

Just the continuation of subtle sensations for a little while gets you to equally mindful insights. Surprisingly, even the gross and painful sensations offer wisdom. They both serve the purpose they are meant to serve. A key that opens their potency is when you are unattached to both and do not long for any of these sensations, nor do you wish the absence of any of these — in one word, being equanimous through this process is the required action, without which all your hard work will be set back a few notches.

What is the big deal of getting into that that gap/ space? Why try all this? This seems to me an innate desire of human consciousness that we are born of light frequencies or beyond. I could not even comprehend what or where the other trains might be heading, but they are at faster and subtler frequencies, for a world beyond my present imagination, but I am sure the makers and writers of films like *The Matrix, Avatar* and such sub-human series have got insights into this.

So, you are the light and well on the path of being the source of illumination for those who do not see it yet. With all this happening, there is one old acquaintance who sticks around. It is none other than Ego.

The Ego & Ideas

You have read about the cell. It was a cell of liberation and insights. One of the insights that came to me initially came in as a feeling. I was overwhelmed by a feeling of sadness washing over me. It was as though I had just enjoyed getting wet in the rain and as far as that great experience went, the clothes had become heavy, my boots were all soggy and pulling me down. As I kept meditating, the reason of that sadness manifested as a thought. "Will you be sacrificing me for the sake of this meditation that you are undertaking? Can't you see that I will not be there if you continue on this path? Are you willing to lose me forever?" I remember straightening up and making a squinting expression with closed eyes as to who this 'I' is and who is going to lose whom? Who will cease to be? There was a moment of fear and trepidation as though I was just about to embark on something that would change my life forever. This drama quickly ended when I realised that it was just another form my thoughts had taken — a form of sadness and of physical heaviness. The power of the thoughts was so heavily accented in that closed confined room ... almost palpable anguish.

What came next will stay with me, maybe for a long time or forever. The 'I' that felt threatened was my ego. It reminded me that all through my life, even when I was leading an unaware life, it had nourished me and my life and brought me to this stage. And now, because I had someone more interesting and practical, I wanted to give up on it. The ego brought back all the memories where it had supported me and made my life — the high points of achievement, especially passing college, getting admissions to an engineering college; clearing the Navy exams and interview, and on it went from the beginning of this life till that very moment in the cell. There was an audible sign that escaped my lips. I stayed there in that silence for as long as I could gather my remaining strength, because the body had started to pain again and to a high degree. As I continued, out of nowhere — it's usually out of nowhere isn't it — I had this unexpected analogy: You are thinking you are this tiny light bulb with electricity running through you and you believe that you are illuminating the whole world. But you know deep inside that this is not true.

Because you see so many shadows and dark spots, your illumination is limited and yet you try all the things possible to glow brighter and brighter. You try pushing through all barriers and want to prove that you are the one. What you don't realise is that the electricity running in to make you glow is controlled by someone or something you don't even bother to know for a long time in your life. Secondly, the switch for you can be turned off anytime and all your huffing and puffing, glowing and dimming will be gone in one instant. Aha! I thought that is this 'I', but then there was something more to it. I then pictured that this was not the full story. There was more to it. I could then see that I was one light bulb among an infinite number of light bulbs, all neatly arranged in complete harmony. There was an array of light, which when switched on, could light up an area which I could not even imagine. It was basically infinite. I then saw clearly that what I was doing, meditating, was not to annihilate the 'I' or my ego. It was more to realise that there was a grand scheme of things in which I was just going to merge to give more light; not switched off, but used in a way to light up the path of many others. It was not a snubbing of the ego, but rather an illumination of the whole space where it could fit in and start providing to all.

I also realised that the purpose of the existence of the ego is not bad or to be craved for or to be averse to. Aversion to the ego will only lead us towards more suffering. The desire to relinquish it and to distance ourselves from it might not work. I know the word ego has taken a bad rap, but after this event I see it differently. It is an integral part of me; it has been doing its bit as it is supposed to do to keep me going. If it was so powerful, I never would have embraced on the journey of self-awareness. At the end of the session, I silently thanked the process which was taking me through this journey of consciousness before stepping out of the cell. You cannot imagine the lightness I felt after this. It was as though that very burden that I had been loaded with had been lifted and something like balloons fastened on to me —think of the animated movie *UP* where the balloons lift and fly an entire house to a destination that was once only a dream to the protagonist.

MY IDEA – Concept and conflict

After one of my morning meditation sessions, I had this awesome idea. Immediately, the next thought was that this was MY idea. Through my experiences till this moment I have always used the words, "I have an idea" and owned them. In some instances, I have defended them fiercely. Now, I can only look back and laugh at those memories. The curious thing this time was that somehow these two words 'my idea' did not sink in. I felt I was doing something sacrilegious. The direction in which I was being directed to this time was a new one altogether. So, there was deeper diving required into this 'my idea' concept; and the questions which kept popping up were:

How can this be MY idea? Why can it not be MY Idea?

Who is this ME and the concept of MINE?

Did the body that is assigned to the name Harry produce this idea? How could the body produce it?

Did the brain, which is assumed to be the centre of thought, have this idea? If so, how can this idea belong to the brain? Isn't it just an organ?

These were the questions that kept flashing in quick succession. More in line with Ramana Maharishi's, "Who Am I?" enquiry.

CAUTION: *I don't mean to say that you should/or should not take ownership of the ideas that come to your mind. I would rather have you experience and taste this phenomenon. You would not know the taste of Coffee unless you experience it yourself. So, unless you get on your own path of self-discovery and experience the taste, you would not know.*

The answers did not flash through, although they did come by gradually and over a period of time. Before I got the answers which could be articulated in the language I predominantly used, it was more of a knowing that the ideas were not mine because there was no ME. For some reason, the experience was as though the concept of ME and claiming personal ownership over an idea had taken a walk and left the building unattended.

I realized that all ideas existed and had always been around in the one Universal Mind – just like the air we breathe. It is just a matter of who connects with this Universal Mind and downloads the idea, the message, the story, or whatever you may want to call it. You can liken it to a huge network grid with infinite ideas. The ideas are all floating about and one of the 7.4 billion or any number of the 7.4 billion human receptors (personal minds) can link up to the Universal Mind and receive that idea at that moment.

Of course, you will see the obvious logic. The idea does not differ based on race, caste, creed, class or any of those things, nor does it cater only to so-called labels of rich, poor or physically-fit etc. It is just there. The Mind just gives.

Recently I attended a book reading session. The reason this memory comes to mind is that the author of this book is pretty young — sixteen years old and already written and published his first book. Now we know for a fact that he is the author; however, I am sure his inspiration was his connection to the source. And yes, the Universal Mind is present both for the young and the old. You can connect to this network at any age!

So, as the answers began sinking in gradually, the entire paradigm of taking ownership, defending, expecting praise and a pat on the back for an idea just faded away; it was no more needed. I realized that there was never a need to be bent out of shape if my ideas were not accepted, not praised or are stolen — these statements are based on my corporate experience, having been there and seen others fight it out — because they are not mine in the first place as there is no Mine. It just is. One would call me crazy if I staked claim to the air we all breathe. Similarly, no idea is totally yours. Ideas can come in bits and pieces and be merged by a meeting of the minds. They can be given to many at the same time too; so no point in beating yourself up if others stake claim to it. It is not ours or anyone else's anyway.

THE OUTCOME IS: When there is no ME, there is nothing that is MINE; and when there is nothing MINE, there is no holding on, no grasping, and no resistance. It's like the Zen story, "just imagine you are falling through this world and you see that everything around you is also falling with you."

The wisdom of the sages are true — we are all from the same source and we are all in the mind as forms. The human experience is one of its kind; I am sure when you expand into being nothing, you know that you have always been and will be. There is no end.

The questions that need to be asked is — do you want to be different? Do you want to be recognized? Do you want to gain prestige? Or do you just want to serve by being what you are supposed to be? When a person truly understands the prayer "thy will be done," the prayer of the personal mind will be "thy will be done by me or through me." I'm just a conduit, a channel. The body and its senses are mere tools used to express what life wants to experience and express, ideas being one of them that life experiences.

Try losing the ME and see what happens. It is one amazing ride.

This brings me to the part of questioning and why enquiring is vital on the path to a happy and successful living.

Quality Questions Versus Quality Life

As I continued the arduous and painful journey, I remembered the challenging days I had gone through during my corporate days in the oil and gas industry, especially offshore. Picture this scenario where you are with a team of intelligent, hardworking people with resources available at your disposal, yet you come up against an impasse, a technical hitch that seems so doable but still cannot be overcome with the traditional bookish knowledge which is available.

I recalled one such challenging event during which we achieved a breakthrough with the simple sentence, "silly question time" where my friend, colleague and a Marine captain worked together to achieve what we did. This silly question time became a sacred time. Every time we faced a challenging situation, my colleague used to call for silly question time. What it meant was that three or four of us who were the key drivers of delivering a particular task went into the Chief Engineer's office. Why Chief Engineer, you may wonder? Because he had the best coffee and the best of the coffee machines, which he had somehow coaxed the shore office to purchase for the barge and it sat like a proud trophy in his office.

Anyway, we used to file into his office. Once inside, each got busy making coffee; I was usually clumsy and seemed to have a longish learning curve just to make that machine work and deliver some real good coffee. After having had a sip each and talking about office gossip (again) and having had a nice, fat complaining session of why the other office guys are useless and such, we got down to business. The interesting part was that I used to wear two hats: when on the barge I was totally an offshore mind, but when back in office, I was the office guy. This did give me a great perspective of the difficulties that both ends faced and also the privileges both enjoyed.

Then, Ian used to announce, "Silly question time, guys! What is happening here? What are we missing? Why are we not getting the results that we so desire?" Now, the mind, having had time to be off the solution, focuses for a time and having had time to relax, started churning out responses that were useful. These were moments when the insights started coming up from each one of us. Each of the responses was verified through a brainstorming session, and more often than not, we came up with working solutions.

Having practised the meditation technique I learnt a year ago, I knew I had made progress; however, there still remained certain doubts in my mind. The above recall of my offshore days brought to mind a few questions I had for the instructor at the camp.

1. The mind seemed to have made a picture of the body and every time I am making a run of

observing the bodily sensations from head to toe, the pictures of each part seemed to appear in my mind. So, I wanted to ask the question — Is it ok to have those images appear?

2. Also, I became aware that with the picture that came to my mind, it seemed to have an internal voice, which added a label to that picture **– it prompted imagine- top of the head - label – go to the top.** Was it normal to have a label going along with the image?

3. On this particular day, there seemed to be as though a lot of guests who had come visiting me had left; by guests I mean thoughts and the place they were visiting me at was in my mind. The house (mind) seemed to be very empty; even the furniture seemed to have been taken away and there was literally an echo in the house every time a thought appeared. In this almost-empty house of the mind, there were two voices debating — I labelled them, Jesus and Buddha. I don't recollect their exact dialogues, but it seemed like they were debating as to who was superior. Maybe my catholic upbringing was being represented by Jesus and the last journey of the last three years into the unknown by Buddha. Even though I realised that there was a witness present observing this dialogue in the silence of the almost-empty mind and come up with the conclusion that that the representations were interchangeable

and Buddha and Jesus are one and the same. Anyway, I was not totally convinced about the conclusion, so I brought up my third question. What are these voices doing in my head? I usually had just one voice in my head; so, were these minimal or non-existent debates before? Also, why this emptiness?

With these questions in mind, I paced near the instructor's mini meditation hall at the appointed time for an audience with him. I approached the instructor with reverence with my silly questions that arose from the silly question time and sat down on the nice, little cushion and tiny pillow. I told him that I had a few queries and he silently encouraged me to continue. I listed them out:

1. Is it ok to have those images appear? He said, no, no imagination, no pictures and no visualisation was to be used for the purpose. But then, the mind is a visual machine. It always picks up and creates images, I argued. You have to break the habit and let it run without any visualisation, he stressed. I had to agree with the technique and I knew the mind had the power to run this new command as it could be rewired and reprogrammed. The teacher did say that even though, initially, just for the sake of understating the concept I might have come up with this solution, it should not be continued though.

2. Was it normal to have a label going along with the image? You might have sensed the answer or seen the pattern. The answer was, no verbalisation and no labelling of the process was to be done. The mind has to run its course by itself.
3. What are these voices doing in my head? I usually had just one voice in the head and were they minimal or non-existent debates before? Also, why this emptiness?

His answer was an analogy — "Imagine you are traveling by bus and the bus is moving. You see a lot of trees, buildings, and lots of things passing you by if you are watching out the window. Is it not?" I responded affirmatively. "Those are your thoughts," he said. "Watch them pass by, do not hold on to them, ok?" I replied, "Ok."

"Here is another analogy," he continued to speak. "When you are at home and having a conversation with someone, you might be having the TV running in the background. You might also have the radio and maybe some other people are having a conversation too, right?" I nodded, indicating I could picture this scene. He said, "Those background distractions are your thoughts. They might always be there or at times be reduced. However, you have to know them for what they are and tune them out if you are to have a meaningful conversation with the person you are engaging."

I understood this analogy very well as I use it in my coaching practice too. I recalled a time when one of my clients came to me at an emotionally challenging time. He had just been through a break up with after a couple of years of dating. I asked him to tell me what he was thinking about; tell me about the movie running in his head at the moment. He started telling me of his pain. I re-iterated for him to describe what was playing in his mind. He came up with an accurate description of what was going on; and in an instant saw why he was so sad, upset and angry. I asked him if he wanted to try something different; a different movie perhaps? Given the pain he was going through he reluctantly agreed. Even though I could see that it was difficult for him to relinquish the fascinating movie he had running in his mind, even though he had told himself that the normal response, the culturally-trained response was that of sadness, pain and anguish, he was willing to change this script.

I asked him to now start playing a new movie; this time I specifically asked him to play the movie that made him laugh in life. It could be a real-life event or he was given the opportunity to choose any movie that he had watched which made him laugh. He chose a movie and screened it in his mind. There was a momentary break in his demeanour. His rigidly tense face lost its tension and a smile surfaced just for an instance. That moment I knew he had made the connections to start afresh. When he left I knew that he had undergone a change and was looking forward to his work and life again.

This has happened not just once, but on a few occasions. So, listening to the instructor, I knew the experience and now had it referenced at a deeper level of understanding by experiencing it again in a different situation.

Ha! Just three questions? No, I had a few more which popped up at the end of the course too. They were more technical in nature and pertained to the final instructions that were given for the complete dissolution of the body.

Until then, you too can go on an adventure of yourself. Take the time today to do it.

More questions

When you ask profound questions you get profound answers. Here was one such creative question which I came across as I was writing this book. The question was by author Gregg Braden — "What if this is the last written book left on Earth, to be found once everything else was destroyed?" What message would I love to leave behind?

The answer at the moment I wrote the book was — the message I want to proclaim passionately is, "you don't have to suffer; you can choose a different reality. This different reality is only one moment, one action and one thought away. The Moment is NOW; the action is to Be Aware, and the thought is, I AM!" You can choose to fill in the thoughts here and now; and believe me, that is the reality which will be standing in front of you.

If you choose to say, "I am happy, I am love, I am speed" or whatever it is that brings a smile to your face, then that is what you will have. If you choose a lower frequency of thoughts and their associated words, then that is the reflection you will receive.

Did it get you started? It got me started for sure.

What is your true purpose here?

What if you are a unique being?

What would you do if you had all the money you think you need? What then? What would you do differently?

One of the greatest gifts that we have is the ability to question. If there were no questions, would there have been any answers? Would there have been all the inventions that we now see, the benefits of which we reap aplenty?

Begin by taking time to reflect on the present answers you are receiving from life. The answers are in front of you. The depth of your relationships is an answer. The joy and happiness in your life is an answer. The job satisfaction you have is an answer. The wealth you are manifesting is an answer. The health you now have is an answer.

If the answers are not manifesting into what you really want but are the opposite, then you need to question yourself.

What are my true intentions in life?

What is the one thing I can do to change the present situation?

Reverse Engineering

You must have heard, read and understood about reverse engineering and the market it has captured since the phrase was coined. However, this phenomenon has always been in action. The concept of reverse engineering works because something that has already been working efficiently gets completely deconstructed and put back together again, maybe at a different price though. This deconstruction and re-construction process is done so many times that it can literally be done blindfolded. For the process of deconstruction you have to take each step in the reverse order from the final step. You cannot run from the final step right into the middle part and expect yourself to re-construct the system in the same time and accuracy

Now, where do you see this process in your everyday life? Do you remember building Lego? Deconstructing it, or sometimes, having dropped it to find that some small parts have come out and you cannot put it back again unless you break them down into its smallest components. Or have you had the experience of breaking open your early childhood toy only to find you cannot put it back again the way you deconstructed it? And then the next time you deconstructed the toy, you made note of the sequence of steps and which part went where and found that you have made it!

Have you worked in the software industry, especially in detecting how particular software work and how it could be eliminated as in the case of a virus attack, and studied to prevent them from causing damage.

At the meditation camp, I had observed that the technique of Vipassana had taken me into the depths of my mind, deep within; and in doing so helped in eradicating a lot of unwanted programs that were still running and draining my life force. This life force is meant to be used for purposes aligned with what life wants rather than being dumped into the abyss of no return only to be lost, and in turn, causing grief and misery.

I also observed that the principle behind learning this technique was the age-old wisdom of writing it in one sequence and then retracing the steps in the reverse order in the exact sequence that you went ahead with. Does not mean anything yet? Do you remember learning numbers in your childhood and one of the techniques was that the teachers asked you to recite the numbers in reverse order. Same with alphabets. How about the ingraining of the writing process? Write a letter and then retrace it in reverse. Now I can't forget my numbers, letters and the writing even if I wish to.

If you are a welder or have worked in the ship-building industry, having observed the welding process, you will see this principle at work there too. The first pass of the weld is made; then the back is gouged out, and then, the next pass is made. The result of following this is that the ship's weld lasts longer then the parent metal most often. Back gouging helps remove impurities that might have got lodged.

Moment after moment, I sat there and went through the process of creating a new habit pattern and I used the scientific technique of reverting the flow. The mind was made to flow from the top of the head, observing the sensations from one small part of the body at a time, gradually, in order, step by step, until I found my mind at the tips of my toes, having traversed through each and every part from the tip of the head to the toes. Then, the mind reversed its flow from the tip of the toe and traversed upward to the head one. This was done over the last 6 days of the entire course from the moment I was given instructions to the Vipassana technique until the last day.

What happened as a result is that the process got imprinted in the mind and cannot be dislodged easily, and if I continue a two-hour practice each day over the next year or so, the mind would have perfected this and would work in auto mode without any intervention whatsoever. This is the creation of a new habit pattern. Secondly, as you have seen, the process also eradicates mistakes, impurities and perfects the systems. So, also by going through this process without my thinking or doing away with the impurities that were lodged in between due to life's unconscious or unaware reactions were surfacing and being removed. When this occurs, the mind gets strengthened and its sharp focus lasts for a long time.

How can one use this in daily life?

Say you have a plan, a vision of getting something done. Or even a goal to achieve. Start with the final clear vision of what it is that you would like to see happen. Now you see where you are in the present moment. Build up a tiny part-by-part pictorial, worldly or any other way you feel the sensations associated with those steps. It is important to feel connected to the parts taking you towards the goal. Once you have got to the final destination start the process of deconstructing the plan one small step at a time but in the reverse order. Do this a few times and this new goal that you need to achieve will be ingrained in the mind; and before you know it, the final vision you had in mind has been lived. It usually means that a physical manifestation of your plan is being experienced. Now, what happens is that the resources you need, the events that need to occur, the time required and all fill the space to make it happen for you. Of course, there is action, which is required to be taken, i.e., not only the action of visualisation in the process, but the moment to moment action that you had seen yourself take.

Here is how it worked for me in yoga too. My teacher taught me something called FLOW once a week. In this, we do a set of 12 *asanas* (yogic poses and techniques) going forward, and then, reverse it in the exact same order without missing a beat. The benefits of this once a week FLOW exercise has worked wonders for me personally and it has ingrained the complete set in my mind so securely that even when I am not in the class and travelling or working from home, these steps come to me as naturally as breathing. I don't have to sweat my mind to recollect the steps. It's the same with Suryanamaskar, the basic 12-step sun salutation. Once you have practiced them, they become a part of your mind's hardwiring.

So, begin using this simple yet effective technique to create a new reality. I and my coaching clients have used this and other techniques consistently to manifest changes in their lives.

In the last section of the book you can read of the practical use of the technique and implement it for your benefit.

SECTION 3

80% SUCCESS

Health - Happy Two Feet

One of the first things I saw on entering the meditation campus was a note posted at different locations around the campus that said, "Eyes downcast." Initially, this was a difficult task that specially went against what I was taught — to look up straight and walk like you mean your talk and make your presence felt confidently and powerfully. This outward poise could be a necessity when you are dealing with the world in general and especially in the roles you play as leaders, as role models or for anything that requires a show of strength irrespective of what you might be feeling inside.

Having been trained by the Indian Navy, the discipline of walking with the head held high is ingrained into the mind during those gruelling training months where you are broken down to a functioning human being and then put back together with a tag — Now you are an officer and a gentleman. Even to this day I salute the training and the mental discipline that was instilled into me as an officer. In this new setting though the requirement is to keep looking down, eyes downcast. This causes you to wonder what you are missing, and how submissive you would be looking, meekly walking around, unable to make eye contact and see the eyes of others. Being unable to look into the eyes of another means you don't know the intent of the other person and what is going on in their mind.

A note here is relevant: The reason for the rule to keep the eyes downcast in this environment is not to subdue your value or make you feel worthless or invaluable. I learnt through experience that the reason is to actually to make you see more clearly, not into the eyes of the other person but into yourself. It was to avoid any form of communication with anyone out there. It was to improve your self-worth through the realisation that through the portal of your mind and body, you can experience the purpose of life for you to be here.

Keeping my eyes downcast, I started noticing the gait of the various feet that cross you — take over, stop, shuffle and all types of gestures. You see and learn that each one is a different set of feet of course, but also the movement, the urgency, the deliberateness of the movement start registering and a pattern emerges. You see that there are some feet which are slow, very slow, some are fast, while some look tired. You also notice that not all feet are the same — some of them have seen pain due to the ravages of a childhood disease and they are bent at an unnatural angle. As you see patterns you start noticing that all feet have one thing in common — they are all walking towards or away from something. Some are walking towards happiness and some are walking away from pain. You notice that there is a sudden drop in speed for some of them as they near the meditation cell; on the other hand, you notice vigorous and enthusiastic walking when the meditation period ends. They all have a purpose. They all seemed to be going somewhere. Even when the feet were in one place, sometimes there was minor movement going on all the time. It was all passing into the next moment. It was as though there was a universal purpose: walking into the next moment whether one liked it or not.

It brought back memories of when I had walked myself into various events, situations, and moments like achievements, into sadness, into trouble, into freedom, into bondage and all sorts of things since the time I started walking. The feet appeared to me as a river — ever flowing, ever restless, ever becoming and moving into something. Holding the river still seems a futile task as they are not meant to be held back.

Is it not the way life is? Always flowing from one step to another; sometimes slow, sometimes almost running, sometimes at a standstill. As I continued to keep my eyes downcast, observing where I was going, I could not help noticing that like we identify faces, if seen enough times, you also can recognise the uniqueness of each pair of feet and you also notice that the movement and gait in each person's step varies. Some days they almost seem happy to be doing what they are doing, on other days they seem almost dejected, sad and on the verge of giving up. Some pick up speed as the days progress and some would have lost their initial hurriedness and slowed down as though they were taking in the scene of where they were stepping, as though being pensive and contemplative, becoming mindful of what is occurring within. In short, the feet reflected the state of mind of each person.

There came the deeper realisation that I was associating the learnt responses of the way my feet worked based on situations throughout my life I had mapped my experiences to decipher the pattern in the movement of feet. The feeling or realization that hit home was — we are all on a journey, taking various paths. The journey is what makes the difference and not the end results. You can walk fast, slow, stay rooted to the spot it... all does not matter because wherever you are at that moment is exactly where you should be in life at that moment. Your presence at that point in time is what life wants to experience through you. There is nothing else that really matters.

My feet were one of the most important portals into myself; not just the walking, but when I sat down and started the journey of being still physically. I experienced numbness: to pain and the increased pull of gravity that made my feet and legs weigh like lead. It was as though I was being pulled down really hard. These same feet were also where subtle vibrations like small ripples across a lake occurred; it was in them that I experienced what it was to have the minute, fast, painless vibrations of life coursing through me.

I realised that all feet were marching to an unknown, unheard beat. They were all marching upwards and evolving to walk faster and faster towards liberation — liberation from the almost constant buzz of wanting more, to be happy, the ever-present mental script which has been drilled into each individual mind that it is ok to suffer for the sake of attaining pleasure. The pursuits of pleasure by our happy two feet are an indication that we are walking in the wrong direction.

What gives to change the direction of where we are heading? What is the first step required to be taken?

The first step is that of becoming aware of where we are right now. Where am I? What is the truth of my present state of body and mind? This very first step is the beginning of a new journey and the path it will take will be towards liberation. It is not my place to portray anything pertaining to enlightenment or the big philosophical goal of attaining nirvana. The simplicity of becoming aware of where you are right now is aligned to what life is heading towards. I believe Eckhart Tolle when he says the human consciousness is evolving at a rapid pace now and evolving towards a new world order. It should not be treated as a doomsday or rapturous climax. I see it as happening now as well as being drawn into an infinitely long time and space capsule, which being infinite could very well be just a point; a moment without any space and time constraints. In a nutshell, we are experiencing what life wants to experience through us right now. The present experience is for more and more of us to experience the intangible free from material manifestations

You are not walking alone on this path; in addition to you walking towards living an aware life there is something walking towards you. Let's call it Grace. The speed by which grace walks towards you is directly proportional to the effort you put in to live a life aligned to the purpose destined by life for you. One of the ways to know if you are living your life's purpose is to ask yourself what you are passionate about and whether you are living enough to live out that passion. Are you really putting in enough effort to live and breathe doing what you really love doing? Oh! By the way, without getting into a long chapter of disclaimers, note that putting in effort and destroying other lives and decimating this world is not something which is propelling you towards liberation, rather it is exactly the reverse. So, for the sake of god, embrace passions that serve others and enhance the life of others, is what I am referring to, not the fanatical passion of destruction of this world. Wonder what would happen if there was no yardstick to measure this.

When you become aligned to life's purpose for you, often there seems to be a mysterious pull towards becoming healthier and you start focusing on keeping the body fit. See how that works.

Walking Towards Health

I am reminded of the time I was out watching the movie *Inferno* with my wife. For some reason, Tom Hanks' remark on doorways got me thinking about door bells. I became aware of the number of times I have heard a doorbell ring — I am either opening the door when it rings or I am the one doing the ringing.

What got me excited was that doors represent opportunities. So, I am either asking people to give me new opportunities by engaging with them; sometimes opportunities are ringing the doorbell. The interesting part in this excitement is that some of the doorbells have led to opening of some amazing, life-changing and fulfilling experiences. One of the most prominent of these experiences occurred in March, 2016. I was standing outside the door and ringing the bell of my yoga guru so he would open the door for me. It was the first meeting to discuss what I wanted and what he could do for me. I had just arrived from Malaysia and was starting to set up a life in India. That door opened into a completely different world of awareness, fitness and flexibility. I am so glad I rang that bell because now, every time I am on the other side of the door ringing a door bell, visiting family or friends who I have not met for some time, this is what happens. They open the door and the first thing they notice and comment is, "Harry, what is with you? You look so fit and slim! How did you get to this state?" I am in a state of gratitude and I thank my yoga guru for his efforts and the transformation.*1

Here is what happened and how I went about losing 12 kilos in 4 months. When I joined the yoga class, one of the important activities is, of course, the yoga and the various *asanas*; however, what really helped me were three key transformation points:

One was the personal life story of my yoga guru. In short, he had an accident and went through a year of incredible, debilitating pain, unable to stand or walk. From that state of complete incapability to starting his own yoga school by the power of his mind and yoga is inspiring. Of having lived through the ordeal, he now lives to **inspire people** to live a better and healthy life. This is selfless service and giving back to the community.

Secondly he asks all his students to keep a food dairy because many of the students want to lose weight. It helps people be mindful of their eating habits. In my case, it was more for flexibility than to lose weight — I was not obese, just a little overweight at 76 kg ... Who am I kidding here! By now I had read four different books on weight management. One of the books that I had followed to the letter and lost weight before was Gary Taube's *Why you are fat and what you can do about it*. I recommend this book to most of my friends because it is well written and the principles work. Anyway, somewhere down the line I had lost sight of the purpose. I slid into the comfortable rhythm of eating happy food, which in my case was rice, rice and a little more rice. So here I was, with yoga classes and after two weeks I went with my food dairy to my guru. He looked at it, circled the foods that I should avoid, then looked up at me and said, "Harry you are eating the right type of food, but I would like you to include salads and make them 30–40% of your meal portion." That was all. That is the only time I actually showed him my food dairy, because after that instance, it was as though the mind unlearnt the habits that were creating unhealthy choices and moved towards creating healthy choices mindfully. This is what a coach can do. One moment of clarity that brings about a life-transforming change. In this instance, he brought me back to being mindful. Going forward, my meditation practice helped me achieve mindfulness. **So, the second key was Mindfulness** — of what I was reaching out to eat and putting into my mouth. When you take this action of reaching out to food very consciously, every time consistently, then noticing it by itself is enough for your mind to tell you whether you should eat or refrain from it. In addition, there must be consistency, also in clocking in an hour of yoga a day, even on weekends. This is a potent combination which leads to unbelievable changes. My guru never misses an opportunity to remind me, "Harry it was you, your consistency of sustained effort that has led to these results."

The third important awareness is the **type of food to eat**. Going on a low carb diet and sticking to it and knowing what food is low on carb is easy these days. I personally use **fatsecret.com** whenever I am in doubt of the carb content of the food.

The questions I get is, "how can you survive by not eating carbs?" Most often, the misconception is that carbs are only in rice, roti sugar, noodles, bread etc. The truth is that that even fruits and vegetables contain complex carbs that are a healthier option than simple carbs that are in rice and roti. So, after 4 months and converting the transformation points into a process, I am at 64 kg, flexible and fit. This was one of my intentions and part of the vision board that I created 6 months ago, which has been successfully manifested. Anyone can get to this state with a little bit of courier work and ringing door bells.

Apart from the lessons in living a healthy life and losing weight, you can see that there is a deeper lesson here. How many times have you not rung a doorbell fearing what would be on the other side? Or there might have been times when you have heard the bell and let it go quiet without opening the door. Life waits on either side of the door with its amazing transformative experiences. The first step required though is from within.

Now, it's your turn to use mindfulness to get fit!

Lose the Weight - Mind & Body

What does being healthy mean to you?

What if I told you that being healthy is in your inherent capacity?

Know that you can achieve whatever it is you focus on.

What if I told you that you can manifest all that you want for a healthy living now, over the next few weeks, 1 year, 5 or even 10 years?

Are you clear, certain and specific about what you want?

What if I told you that you already have the resources and skill to get what you wanted? Are you aware that you are resourceful?

The thing is, you might not be aware that you can achieve your dreams, and thus, your results. This could be because you are stuck with a thought pattern that does not allow you to think beyond the narrow and limited thinking. This pattern has been programmed over many years by environment, culture, society, systems, and of course, people.

To begin the journey towards success you must understand that it is not success that brings you happiness, but happiness is what leads you to success.

In other words, you have to have fun along the journey every moment as you work towards your 'success'.

This blueprint gives you a general roadmap towards your success:

1. What is your present state? Take the test.
2. How satisfied are you with your present state of health?
3. Develop your top 5 health goals. Visualize them. Feel them. Live them.
4. Identify the top 5 actions you will take over the next 66 days. Create new habits.
5. Your health affirmations.
6. Your health board.

So, start with step 1

Step 1: Rate each item below from a scale of 1 to 5. How true is it for you? The more you are clear about it, higher is the rating.

1 2 3 4 5

Less True More True

#No	Statement	Response (1–5)
1	I am very clear that I am passionate of living a healthy life.	
2	I have a clear list of health goals.	

3	I spend time working on my health.	
4	I sit quietly and observe my thoughts and pay attention to my body talking back to me.	
5	I have experienced moments of clear inner guidance and taken action based on that inner guidance.	
6	I feel confident, resourceful and know that I have all the skills that I need to be healthy.	
7	I notice that there are important areas in my life related to my health not only of the body, but also the mind.	
8	I know and feel that now I am ready to explore ways of developing myself mentally and physically.	
9	I trust that the universe is directing me towards living a healthy life which includes health of mind, body and soul.	
10	I am a strong person and dedicate time, energy and finances to identify changes required and to implement them.	

Step 2: Major Health Areas - Are you satisfied?

A) Rate each item on a scale of 1–10 of your satisfaction level. Choose the one score that best represents your feelings, thoughts and behaviour. This time only for health.

S. No	Major Area of Life	Present Satisfaction level	Attention given Rating	Time Spent Rating
1	Health of Body			
2	Health of Mind			
3	Health of Soul			

B) Rate each passion for the amount of time you are spending doing it/living it. On a scale of 1 to 10, with 10 being the most times in a day.

It goes without saying. If you are not satisfied that means you will have to give it more time.

C) Rate each of the passions according to the attention you are giving each passion. On a scale of 1 to 10, with 10 being the most times in a day. Do you want to improve your health? Are you willing to give it more attention?

D) Identify your present habit patterns which are associated with your present health condition and satisfaction level.

What time of the day do you wake up?

What do you feed your body?

What do you feed your mind?

What do you feed your soul?

NOW answer the further following questions:

What are you willing to do when you decide to give time and attention to health in your life?

Which habits are you willing to change in order to attain peak performing health?

Step 3 & 4: Create your top 3–5 goals for your health. Assign 3 to 5 clear actions which you will take to reach your goals over the next 66 days.

S. No	Goals	Action
1		
2		
3		
4		
5		

Step 5: Your health affirmations

A) See what you see, hear what you hear, feel what you feel. Let your imagination go full throttle; no brakes.

Start with the sentence: WHEN MY LIFE IS IDEAL, I AM…

1.

2.

3.

4.

5.

Some examples

I am at the perfect _____Kg of weight.

I am running ______Km per day.

I am a walking _______.

I am eating ______.

I am aware of my thoughts.

I am spending time taking care of my soul.

We all have used, heard or come across vision boards. Vision boards are powerful tools to program your mind. You can create a health board for yourself. I have used a vision board with the belief in the universal law of attraction for a long time now and believe in its potency. Join me in manifesting your perfect health.

Step 6: Health Board

Create your vision board

Use any vision board builder free app and create your vision board.*2

Collect pictures; could be your personal pictures or from the net to align and represent each of health affirmations.

1. Open the vision board builder and insert all these images one at a time onto the builder.
2. Rearrange the pictures as per your creativity
3. Insert the affirmation as text onto your vision board.
4. Print copies of the board in high colour and have it displayed prominently at places where your attention goes often.

When you are fit and healthy, you have true wealth. When you have true wealth, you might be inclined to share. How can you go about sharing and serving?

Released from Service

It was just another ordinary day. I had served the Navy for seven years and now the time had arrived for me to pursue the path that I had chosen. I had chosen to quit the service and wander along the dreamy path of "seeing the world," which was what prompted me to join the Navy in the first place. The official document read 'released from service.' A quiet severance and a relationship of seven years got over. Just like that, I was not an officer anymore; I was no longer a gazetted officer. I was a retired officer at the young age of 29. For some reason, there has never been any emotional charge to this walking out from one profession into the space of a corporate job and hopping around places in Southeast Asia, West Asia and Europe.

This too was just another ordinary day. The last day of my second Vipassana course was just getting over, I had stayed put for the 10 days, unlike the first course, and surprisingly, I had not made this one a determination of staying put for 10 days. As it always is with hindsight, the days had flown by swiftly. The river kept changing every moment and here I was, staring at the new river every day. The contours holding the river seemed to tell me what was coming next, yet everything kept changing. I felt alive in a quiet way, not the jumping up and down kind, or the shouting kind or any shouting at the top of the voice kind. Here too there was no emotional charge; just a quiet ending of one moment of life, albeit this moment got measured as a 10-day block of time. This too had passed as the other moments had. The difference was that now I did not feel "released from service," rather, "released to serve." It was as though the big blocks of time over the last 39 years were masterfully crafted to take shape into something useful and not just to myself anymore. There was no seeing the world dream here, but just a subtle feeling that my purpose was to serve; all this while was a giving and serving of a different kind and now it was going to be more direct.

As I walked the circuit earmarked for participants to get their daily walk, I met Agni — of course, the name's changed — one of the young participants who had been part of the same 10-day course as I. Being the day of 'preparing to meet the world', we were allowed to interact. So, we got talking and he asked me what I did. I gave him my 5-minute spiel of being a life coach and how I woke people up to rediscover their dreams and live their passions. "That is good," he said. As we got talking, he shared about his passion for serving people and wanted to do it in the way of taking a shot at the Indian Administrative Services exams, clearing them and serve to make people's lives better. He asked me how I could help.

This is where it got interesting for me. There have been moments where I have seen clients grapple with the concept of living their dreams driven by their top passions. At times they have found that this was way too much in the future and that it sometimes became an attachment with clients and they lost their sense of the present and got fixated on goals that became part of living their passions. Although I knew it intellectually and by personal experience that this was not the case, I had never created a vision for a Vipassana meditator. This was interesting because after the 10 days at such a camp you had experienced the reality and importance of the present moment so powerfully and consistently over the days that anything linked to living for a future goal seemed meaningless and outright contradictory. So was it with "If I make any goals I am craving for it, is it not," he asked. I paused for a few minutes. This is where I again experienced the teaching of an entire course in miracles in a split-second.

"You cannot teach what you have not learnt, and what you teach you strengthen in yourselves because you are sharing it. Every lesson you teach you are learning."

What I was about to teach was something which I had experienced. Making goals did not mean that you are going to crave for them in such a way that if not achieved you will become miserable. By hiding behind the curtain of craving you might have passed up many instances to serve or achieve the purpose of life itself. It is not the goals that are the problems. It is the attachment to the outcome which drives the scale of misery. The more you want the results to be exactly how you have planned, the way you have imagined, the more miserable you become when none of the outcomes nor the milestones are aligned to the way you imagined it. This is an important lesson. You can have a huge goal, and want it to happen too, but you cannot decide the 'how' of it. Life itself will make your goal manifest, maybe in a way you least imagined. So it is important to be clear of what you want, but not bother much about the how; having said that, it does not mean you take no action whatsoever to get to that point. So, with this brief explanation, I got to work.

I asked him to create the vision of what it would be like to have cleared the exam. He did. I then asked him to describe what he pictured and his sensations on the body associated with that picture. "I had seen the whole scene clearly and I had some subtle sensations on the body," he replied. I said, "Now forget about what happens in the end. Your imagination was done in the present moment. Your picture was as real to you as it would be as though it was happening in reality and your body manifested it now. So, it is that when you picture this at any given time, using any of the tools you use, be it a vision board, an affirmation, or just plain imagination or review your study goals; it will be done in the present moment with the intensity and sharp focus your mind has been tuned to with this technique of meditation. The thing is not to be attached to it and run a mental movie marathon of reactions." Agni seemed satisfied with this approach.

This small lesson is vital in achieving your goals. The clearer you become of what it is that you want, easier becomes the path to manifest it in the physical realm. The sensations on the body are such powerful pointers, which when used appropriately, can pave the path to your dreams with happiness. It comes in very handy when you want to change behaviour. If you can imagine the new behaviour or habit pattern clearly in your mind and hold on to that image or picture such that there are equal and appropriate sensations corresponding to that image being triggered, then you are programming your mind to believe that the new habit pattern or behaviour is already being lived. The physical ramifications of the new pattern might not be visible right away; however, the process of change has already started and you will see it.

This is to serve, and serve selflessly, so that others might go on to live their dreams of serving even more people in turn. The power of being fully present and aware of every form that the moment takes is liberating. Only this one step can transform you to live so vibrantly and fully. Now, imagine you taking the next step of observing the form the present moment has taken and not reacting to it as wanting more of it or wanting it to disappear. Combined together, this process is the moment-to-moment living on the path to liberation.

As you march towards the new beat of life, which is leading you to serve, having clear intentions brings a sense of enthusiasm. What are intentions anyway?

Intentions are Power Thoughts

How to Use Intention and Focus

When you begin to focus your attention on a particular intention, you can start seeing the actual physical manifestation of that intention. The word 'intention' caught my attention when my friend, now mentor, asked me, "State your intentions more clearly." Such a short sentence and it stopped me in my tracks. It caused me to pause and reflect on all that I had been planning. This event occurred when I was going through a period of dynamic transition from a full-time paid job to becoming self-employed. It was one of the turning points in life that guided me to achieve what I had mentally conceived. As Napoleon Hill once said, "Whatever the mind can conceive and believe, it can achieve." I achieved this by focusing my attention on the clear intentions that I had developed. You too can conceive and achieve any possibility using your mind by developing clear intention and focusing on them. The sharp focus of the mind that you develop through the meditation practise goes a long way to make this happen.

So to use intention and focus you begin with:

- Stating clear intentions.

- Intentions that are aligned to your passions and not egocentric.
- Develop an action plan.
- Focus – Pay attention to your intention and the action plan that has sprung out of that intention.
- Fully experience the manifestation of your intention.

What is an Intention? Wikipedia states, "Intention is a mental state that represents a commitment to carrying out an action or actions in the future."

The Merriam Webster dictionary gives the meaning as "the thing that you plan to do or achieve: an aim or purpose."

Let's explore in little more detail the steps to use intention and focus.

Stating clear intentions - The first and foremost step in manifesting is to have a purpose an aim. For instance, one of my clearly-stated intention is to spend an hour or more in meditation every day. You could have different intentions. Some of you might be looking for financial success. You could use the six-step process*3 given by self-help author Napoleon Hill in his book *Think* and *Grow Rich*. Or you might have an intention for a brand new car. You are only limited by your beliefs and imagination while developing your intentions.

In the last section we understood how limiting beliefs create a constraint in the flow of life — one of the coaches I know works with people to overcome their limiting beliefs. I mention this because he does it by making them walk on fire. When a person who had a belief that walking on fire was impossible does that impossible task without getting harmed, a shift or breakthrough happens. Imagine what happens to many of the other limiting beliefs? I am not suggesting you walk on fire by yourself. The process of identifying these limiting beliefs and knowing about their existence will help you overcome them.

It is necessary though to look at them objectively, else you can come to bear all the powerful intentions yet see no results because of the neutralising effect of your belief systems.

Once you have the intention in your mind, work with it. If you are a visual, person take time to imagine what this will look like as if it is occurring at the present (which is now), you can also use pictures or paint it. Write it down. During your active imagination you can also feel the emotions that arise as you achieve this. Use the mind. It has unlimited power.

Then what?

Carry out some checks: Are your intentions ego-driven or unfolding as per life's purpose?

Eckart Tolle puts it beautifully in one of his Q&A sessions: "The ego comes not from fullness, but from neediness; from a sense of 'not enough', and that is the ego desire. The ego says, 'I desire that car because I will really feel better when I am sitting in that car and driving it – especially if other people see me in it.' Without other people it doesn't really work. It only begins to work for the ego if other people have cars that are not like yours, the same with a house or anything else that you acquire, any possession. You can perfectly enjoy a nice house or nice car without the ego deriving any pleasure from it, or enhancing itself."*5

Also check out if your intentions lines up with what you love doing. For instance, if you are not passionate about becoming wealthy, then having an intention to be a millionaire will not get through. I found Janet Attwood's book *The Passion Test**6 powerful and useful to understand passionate living. You can take a quick passion test to discover your top passions.*7

Develop a goal-driven action plan: There is a lot of information and data available on goal setting and planning. You can use an app or tool or just write down the goals and plan in your journal. When you develop your goals, keep them SMART. **SMART** Stands for: Specific-Measurable-Attainable-Realistic-Time based.*8.

Another important note here is to create well-balanced goals. Having only future-centric goals with no regard to goals of the present, will create a gap between what is and what you want.

Finally, put the plan in action: While putting your plan in action, pay attention to it — FOCUS on it. In Neuro Linguistic Programming (NLP),*9 one of the presuppositions reads, "What you focus on expands" and "I create my own reality"; The key is focus by giving it your mental time and your energy in executing actions — focus by living the intention each day.

Finally, you will experience the intention that you created as a physical manifestation. A note here: It is crucial that you enjoy the journey. If you develop a craving and attachment to the end result, then there is a tendency to cause resistance along the way, which will lead to suffering. Therefore, it is important to be securely anchored in the present moment as you get on this amazing exercise of using intention and focus.

It would be interesting to note that what was first an intention in my mind – to be self-employed, has been successfully achieved. I moved from a full-time job in Malaysia to India and happily living the intention. I take time to thank life and the people who have been with me along this journey.

So, here is wishing to best for those who are just starting. If you need more details or would like to have a chat about the process feel free to drop me a line or call me. As you swing along this journey of creating high impact intentions, there is an all-important action which needs to be happening ceaselessly. I could have mentioned it in a paragraph here; however, the importance of that action is invaluable and needs special focus and attention.

Appreciate and Thank Life

I love reading books! Especially books on self-help and spirituality. I noticed that in almost all the books, the word 'gratitude' is generously present and has been given prime importance. The common underlying message is — ***live life with gratitude***. On researching the word gratitude, I found that the internet is full of blogs and articles that draw attention to the importance of gratitude in life. It shows that there is an intangible power in living life with gratitude.

This chapter is more of a thank you note to all the researchers, bloggers and writers who have made the miracle of gratitude known to so many. This chapter is also about how gratitude is changing my life each moment.

If we start expressing gratitude to one person at a time, one moment at a time each day, that will begin to bring about a huge transformation of the collective consciousness. The transformation is to live without fear. As American physician and psychotherapy pioneer Carl Whittaker says, "Success is letting go of fear. Your state of gratitude attracts the power of the universe's love towards you. So, begin by expressing deep gratitude for yourself as the first person and the chain reaction will start."

The first thought to write about gratitude occurred to me when I was having a walk among the tree-lined paths back from my yoga class. I realised that I have been grateful to life for a long time now. One of my unceasing prayers has been — *Thank You, Life for directing my path, for instructing and advising me.* I took this as a prayer around a decade ago and since then I have been at it. With hindsight I can say that this was one of my most prominent self-talk. This self-talk had become second nature to me, especially during the times of heightened mental chatter. It helped me as one of the tools to focus on the present moment. I can now look back and see that this has been a source of infinite energy through all my life experiences and taught me to align my present with life's purpose. It has led me through both challenging as well as happier times; more so through the tough moments of the past. I have truly experienced what German theologian Meister Eckhart says, "If the only prayer you said was thank you that would be enough."

The interesting and transformative part that occurred to me is this thought that struck me during my walk. Who offers this gratefulness? Who is that we are showing gratitude to? Is it just a self-talk or something deeper? These questions led me to one of life's amazing experiences of feeling peace and tranquillity; of course, there were no words describing this at that point. I could only feel it as a state of being. This state of being is actually in tune with the energy of the universal source. It has the power to transform life. I realised that words were inadequate to express the deeper meaning. Life is actually celebrating and rejoicing when you are in the state of gratitude. When life rejoices through you, it creates a space for happiness in you and for others who come in contact with you.

So then, let us get on with it and explore gratitude; why it is important and how can we live in a constant state of gratitude? We all say thank you often. One of the early lessons taught to us is to say thank you and please often. If you are practicing this lesson with reverence, then you are already on the path. If not, read on:

What is the meaning of Gratitude?

The Cambridge dictionary's definition of gratitude is "the feeling or quality of being grateful. Being grateful means 'showing or expressing thanks.'"

The book, *A Course in Miracles* says, "What is Heaven but a song of gratitude and love and praise by everything created to the Source of its creation?"

Why is Gratitude so important?

Don't take my story. There are hundreds of success stories around the world where life has been transformed from one of being challenging to that of peace and abundance just practicing the act of showing gratitude to life every day. This one *365 grateful**10 here is an amazing life-changing story. It also shows how you can make life colourful with pictures depicting moments and means of showing gratitude.

There has been research in this field, which shows how gratitude works. So it suffices to know that science backs up this non-physical intangible power. You can read more of this in *Science behind Gratitude*.*11

How to practice gratitude

I found this Ted Talk by David Steindl-Rast clear and helpful.*12 He talks about how each moment or the present moment is full of opportunities and why we can and should use this richness of life and avail of these opportunities by paying attention to the present instead of rushing through life. He ends it wonderfully by saying, "A grateful world is a happy world."

Keeping a gratitude journal is one of the key tools often repeated as advice. I personally have been using the app *Bliss* as my personal gratitude journal.

You can also use gratitude cards that can be prominently displayed.*13

One of the other ways is by making a gratitude list.*14

Here is one of my personal experiences of transformations: A decade ago, I embarked on a journey of gratitude through self-talk not knowing the immense potential of the state it brings about. Just holding on to the thought of gratitude transformed my life.

I started being grateful during a time when I was utterly frustrated and dejected. I was going through a challenging and difficult work place situation. I had moved to West Asia/Middle East for a new job. When I arrived on the site, I noticed that the work I was expected to do was different from what was actually described to me for a marine engineer. This mismatch led to strained relations at work with the management team and frequent arguments. This challenge was becoming too much for me to tolerate; however, I had to continue and give this a fair shot as this was my only source of income and I was literally warned about the drastic consequences of quitting the job in the Middle East before a year was over. It was usually a ban from entering the country; or for a period of one year, minimum.

It was during this time that I was drawn to The Bible and specially the verses that were giving thanks to God and asking for wisdom. I kept wondering how I can thank God during this crisis, but the more I continued just saying thank you, my life seemed to change on its own. I was led by the hand, so to say, to have no fear and negotiate my release from the job. Even as this crisis was unfolding and not yet over, a new beginning was starting. A consultant approached me to work for a MNC. This job offer changed and transformed my life. The years I spent working at the MNC saw my career grow exponentially. Now, when I think back, it was the transformative power of gratitude that led me to a breakthrough by helping me lose my fear — the fear created by my own limited thinking.

Now, how are you expressing your gratitude?

The most important step for you to take is start saying Thank You now, if you are not already doing it.

You can choose one of the many ways to start. Rest assured that life will lead you towards a state of abundance through this simple, transformative step.

The best way to show gratitude is through what feels right for you. You can pick and choose any process or method; the most important yardstick is to feel that state of gratitude.

I have provided some more links in the References Section*15 for you to read and develop your gratitude muscle. As you exercise this, the stronger it will become. You will manifest abundance proportional to the strength you build.

May you live happily and abundantly — the concluding part of every prayer, and in this case, the meditation session was to enable one give compassionate love to other beings. It is called *Metta Bhavana*. When you have flooded yourself with self-love and kindness for yourself and are in a state of gratitude, you will feel the outpouring of your kindness and love to all beings. When you give, you receive many times more.

As you continue to live happily and abundantly you will notice that you are being blessed with the gifts of insights.

Living from Insights

The more I delved deeper into the realm of insights the more I was experiencing them. It is true when it's said that what you focus on grows.

During the 10 days at the meditation camp, I had experienced the power of focus, learnt the art of how to concentrate and applied it to dissolve so many of the hard, knotted, solidified bonds of the mind and body; I knew this was working. As a result of the dissolution there was an immense release of energy, an energy that took various forms; and one of the forms it took was the instant download of information.

Typically I always used to think that any information would be given to me when I read, through words spoken and through the channels I always had gathered information from. Our communication channels are limited to listening through our ears and reading through our eyes and touch, as in pain or pleasure, which is felt through taste and smell. Now, the major chunk of information is through the channels of the two senses — the eyes and ears. Think about it! How else do you gather more information? This data or information then forms the basis of making decisions that stem from the existing memories of events which closely resemble the new information that the senses are gathering. The mind is sharp enough to make comparative computations in the blink of an eye and be ready with an answer for any query or otherwise.

Now consider this scenario. You have been reading for a long time; you have been so hungry for a particular topic that you have been devouring book after book, article after article for years. You suddenly realise that this lifetime is not enough for you to keep reading every day for a few hours and yet consume all the great information from the books. You have come to an impasse. You feel so dejected that you conjure up a crazy wish. Would it not be fantastic that the wisdom of the ages was stored as an instant data download, which when connected by a certain frequency, the entire data is instantly downloaded into the human mind from the mind like we had seen in films such as *The Matrix* and the lot.

This is what exactly happened to me just before I headed for the second Vipassana retreat. I was sitting down and reading *The Impersonal Life* and as I went through it I had some really crazy moments as though the book, which was written in 1944, was waiting for me to pick it up, maybe sooner but anyway at least finally, I laid my hand and eyes on it and read it. After reading, I was stunned that I wanted to gain so much knowledge through more reading that I had always been doing over the last 25 years. I wanted it all, but realised that this lifetime was just not enough.

So, what next? Yes, as you have connected the dots already and seen the connection, we already have this invention; it works and has been working forever. The wisdom of the world has always been there. The ideas all exist already. It's just a matter of one moment when you get to realise that all along your life there have been numerous instant downloads. Now bear in mind that these downloads are unlike the way we normally give and receive information that is not through the channels of the eyes, ears and the other 3 senses — This wisdom to live life and make decisions that are more far-reaching is given thus as insights.

I know that being aware that you are working from insights is a tangible manifestation or proof as you may want to call it, of being connected to the divine. And once you are aware, you are working on that plane; and living at that level, you are propelled so to sail towards destinations which you never imagined existed. You gather an immense amount of momentum depending upon your inherent potential you have carried into this world from your past. This momentum carries you, as if in a big hurry, towards the evolution of your mind, to be released and dissolved into the oneness of the great collective mind. The drop has merged with the ocean. The single bulb is now glowing with the source illuminating the whole.

Insights are those moments of clarity which occur to you when you have been silent; and when you have let go of your intense desire to find solutions to problems. Look out for the unbiased small voice which might even speak from within as a guiding light to your life's path.

As you spend more ‘mat time’ or ‘chair time’ doing nothing, you will be able to connect to the collective or universal mind at will and communicate, where exchange of ideas and solutions take place. These insights will drive a lot of your actions in this world of form. One such necessity in the world we live in is financial freedom.

Financial Stability

So you have become aware of yourself, you have also realised that the present moment is all there is. In addition to this, you now have experienced that everything is in a state of continuous flux — everything is passing — it is all impermanent; and because of this, you have experienced the balance which comes as part of it. You equanimously observe the moment to moment evolution of life in the vibratory quantum field.

Meditation has led you to become present to yourself and taught you the art of observing. You have experienced the power of the mind and how it can help you or not by creating habits which either align to your life's purpose or are contrary to them. It makes sense to insert a comment here — *There is nothing inherently right or wrong if you are living life's purpose or not. It's just that sooner or later the resistance will end and life will flow. It could be in this lifetime or maybe some other lifetime. So, don't sweat it.* ***At this moment you are where you should be and who you are supposed to be.***

There are various benefits of meditation as you have seen — but the prominent one so far has been knowing that you are your own 'Mind', and using a laser-like focus of the mind here and now lead to improved relationships and a walk towards great health. This is true wealth.

This also leads to the creation of financial stability if that is what you want. The ability to focus your mind in a single, determined line affects energy in such a way that when such energy manifests into matter, it is close to what you have rehearsed in your mind.

Today, money has taken on epic proportions in terms of importance in our lives, and has almost become the symbol of happiness. Any amount of convincing or cajoling you to think otherwise would be folly on my part. This does not change the fact though that abundance of money is not what makes people happy nor the absence of it is what makes them unhappy. It is one's state of being which makes one happy or not.

As a philosophy this is all good, but when it comes to the task of putting food on the table, paying the bills for the house, ensuring the kids get a decent education, and for you to get your vacation and much-needed relaxation, money is the currency that the world uses; and it becomes imperative that you have it. The lessons that came to me about financial freedom are simple, yet make an impact. I am using them effectively and so can you. These are by no means any guidelines for investment nor are they expertly researched. But they do manage to serve as a firm foundation and an established path that has been in use for a while now.

It all started with an intention in the form of a quality question: How can I become financially stable and how can I weather the uncertainties that crop up every now and again?

I first looked at the amount of money I make and what was going away in terms of expenses. I also created a budget with a clear forecast of how much would be required at the current spend. So, here's Step 1:

1. **Create a budget.**

   Then, I looked at the priority expenses per month and year. Most importantly, I saw a list of debts emerge from this observation. I listed down the debts that I had with the pending amounts, years left to pay and penalty details for each of them. So, in this case, Step 2 would be to:

2. **List down your debts. All of them.**

   After the list was made, I put in place a plan to become debt-free within the next 2 years. I realised it was very easy to get into debt, but very hard to come out of it. It is like a smoker's dilemma. You get into it easily and have lots of fun early on. When the repercussions hit back, you are hit hard and you don't know how to come out of it. You become dependent, and at times, die trying to get out.

   As I was contemplating my debts, the various insurance policies suddenly looked like they were not giving any valuable ROI and they were made with inadequate understanding at the time I bought into them. I put these down into a list with a detailed analysis of how much each policy would pay off, dates when they would mature, the minimum number of years to pay for them without losing any money, and the earliest I could cash them without attracting any penalty and also the maximum benefit you could get with minimum years of paying in. Therefore, Step 3 was in front of me:

3. **List down all the existing investments that you might have, which are a big draw on your earning capacity but are not going to pay any great ROI.**

Out of nowhere, a sudden emergency hit me and the family; I lost my job in a foreign country. This is a constant fear a lot of salaried people live in. You might have experienced something on the lines of an emergency. It could be a sudden illness, a travel plan that came up out of the blue. Emergencies can be of any kind. What I learnt was that it is vital to have an emergency fund at all times ready to be used. I had saved an amount which could last for 2 months when such an emergency hit. Two months are not enough. A minimum of 6 months sustenance needs to be kept somewhere far, yet reachable when the situations warrant. This brings us to Step 4:

4. **Keep an emergency fund.**

Once the above actions are taken towards achieving financial stability, and delivering results towards it, then the intention should move towards creating wealth, investing, buying a house and giving to causes that would bring a smile to your face. Through all this action, being and living, the core of your being is nourished through the relationships you have and live.

Relationships - The Butterflies

As I continued my hour after hour of sitting quietly — not so quietly though — there was quite a lot of squirming, changing positions, yearning for breaks and all that drama going on inside; however, there was something like a clean-up taking place. As though the glass windows through which I was looking at life were being cleaned up. Sometimes, it was so clear I wondered if there was any glass at all through which I was viewing the world. During such moments the beautiful birds and trees seemed magical. The colourful butterflies seemed to be there just to teach me a lesson in love, and about how relationships shape our lives.

The whole fabric of life is woven and the threads are all the relationships in our life. Everything is a relationship. If you fail to see the essence that every relationship comes with its own learning then there is bound to be some friction.

How can you live your dreams if you have no resources? We are wired to think that there is always something required to create something. Well, think again. What about love? You can manifest untold realities through nothing but only love. Love is the most valuable and abundant resource available for us. The catch is, as it goes with most life-giving things, it is not visible — it's like the air we breathe; we cannot see it yet is one of the most vital of resources for us and it is there in plenty for free, unless of course, we confine ourselves to vacuum or a polluted environment.

Our environment for abundance is designed with love available in plenty, just like there were enough flowers for all the different types of butterflies. There was never a moment when I saw the butterflies fighting or striving to possess, or to hoard.

Sitting under the bodhi tree and thinking to myself, "here I am perfectly placed below the bodhi tree. The bodhi tree has gained its popularity by the fact that Gotama Buddha achieved his enlightenment below this tree. I did not become another Buddha ... yet! But what I was taught by nature is an insight that would accompany me through some knotty situations.

All around the tree were these discarded butterfly cocoons. The longer I watched them, the more fascinated I became with this simple yet robust architecture used. Almost evenly cut, pieces of lean sticks- depending upon the size of the caterpillar of-course. Inside this laboured the caterpillar, allowing nature or life or whatever it is you want to call it, to nurture it into the beautiful butterfly that it was to become. It was a beautiful transition that was being manifested inside. The cocoon was protecting the butterfly from predators, from the harshness of life outside. As I watched them over the 10 days during any break time I got between the meditation sessions, I saw that the caterpillars had to go through one of the most challenging periods to become what they became. They literally had to break free from their protective shields in order to continue living and to be the flying colourful ambassadors of nature; to bring cheer to the hearts of the people watching and to help the purpose of nature to help plants pollinate and grow. The lesson was so clear. The old protective sheaths that are formed in early days of our upbringing are appropriately designed and suitable only for that period of time. We suffer at times with these coverings because we think we need them for our living even at a stage when we are ready for metamorphosis and to fly. Those same protective layers become an anchor or coffin. I wondered how many times I had stayed inside with my own creativity, silently carrying the burden of this. Most often, the protective mechanisms are to shield you from other people — people close to you.

Know and thank the protective mechanisms that you have built around yourself for a particular phase in life, but also remember that for your flight you need to break through those layers. How does one do that? By using the power of the mind and the unflinching attitude of letting go and relying on nature — a complete surrender.

I continued my musing and kept watching the flight of the butterflies. Five types of butterflies took to the beautiful flowers and plants around. They were all so distinct from each other, they really stood out. I laughed watching the small yellow ones; they had no sense of direction, no flight plan, they did not even seem to fly. They just bumbled around, and at times, bumping into the thickets and getting caught in the shrub. It reminded me of watching my little daughter learning to walk. She had this uncanny ability as most children do, to walk into obstructions, hit hard, collapse and cry for a bit and then get up and walk again. I could not stop myself from letting this scene flash by in my head. Even through this I knew that there is a purpose to all everything that happens.

The smaller cousins of the yellow ones were the tiny grey ones; they hardly flew, more like hopped from one flower to the other. Then there were three other bigger types, more colourful and really graceful. They seemed to know exactly where they were heading, where the flowers were. They could glide, turn gracefully, had speed and could soar really high.

The patterns I observed in the butterflies seemed so akin to the types of people we have. Some people are just hoping from one flower to the other; some like the yellow butterflies are bumbling through life. Some of us are absolutely goal-driven — we have the skills, beauty, grace, charisma and the style to do things.

The last phenomenon that I observed was that there were times when the wind picked up and the yellow butterflies were taken high up, higher than they could go by themselves, along with the high flyers, in the stream of the wind. I could almost hear them shrieking with glee as they tumbled high up in the air and came back down. In the same way, we too have such spirit — we get the gift of grace at times to be lifted up; high into the realms of absolute joy and glee. Just be and enjoy each moment.

On reading the above, did you identify yourself with a particular butterfly? Did you notice that irrespective of which butterfly you are, you have gone through a metamorphosis process and maybe you are still carrying some of the protective shell which protected you once, but is now redundant.

The common denominator that fascinated me — they all went to the flowers that grew from the earth. No matter how high they flew or how much they tumbled or hopped, they all found the flowers where their resource was. What is our most valuable resource? Love. Where is love? It is in our relationships. Our relationships are our flowers, so irrespective of how high we fly we need to come down, settle down and rejuvenate ourselves, strengthen ourselves to keep moving on. If we do not find nurturing, life-giving relationships in our lives, I think we would all perish or move away in search of refreshing and more nourishing relationships

Did you notice that you too still have to come to the flowers in the garden? Who or what do these flowers mean to you in life? Do they represent your relationships? Do they represent resources that fill you up? Do they remind you of where you can come to when you are tired of all that flying around, tumbling around?

Relationships and Love

If the mind precedes all phenomena, then love is the state of mind that you would want to have as your constant baseline from which your mind can operate. Love is a subtle vibration, a vibration in which peace, harmony, laughter, joy and happiness abide.

My teachers in life have come from relationships I have had — Relations with people, books, nature, things. If you observe closely, you may come up with a few exceptions where your experiences are devoid of relations. So, all of life is one big fabric intertwined together and the intertwining is the relations we have.

I had read this verse, "when the student is ready, the teacher appears." I spent a long time taking this very figuratively and was attached to the word 'teacher' by the image of what a teacher should look like. A teacher, for me, meant a wise person who has experienced life more than I have; an enlightened being. A person who knows something more of what I already know. A person who will lead me by the hand to whatever it is that I have to do in life. Now, only with hindsight, I can say that it was this image that kept me from noticing all the teachers who were right in front of my eyes.

Over the years, I saw that the books which kept coming my way were one of my wise teachers. A divine force kept supplying me with an unending stream of books. When I sat down, one day not long ago, to an inner nudge to see a pattern in the books that had kept coming up, I saw it so clearly. Since the first book I had when I was 14 to this day has been a curriculum designed by an unseen force. From reading comics to keep coming back to books that offered a path towards my spiritual evolution was an 'a-ha!' moment. The clear path that I am being taken on was unmistakably reflected in the books that showed up in my life, and still are popping up. For example, when I was struggling with the decision to join a seminary to become a priest at the age of 14, my good friend and mentor, now a Jesuit priest, handed me two books by Anthony Demello. On reading that, something stirred and for some reason I did not become a priest, but a seed was planted. The seed lay there, dormant for a long time. When I sometimes revisit my past I am reminded of the Mexican proverb, "they tried to bury us, they didn't know we were seeds." I don't know why this proverb comes to mind; maybe because the lessons that I learnt from my friend and the words of Anthony Demello, through his books, lay buried within for a long time and every now and again they must have sensed the ground being prepared for sprouting. One important development from this is — I developed a very intimate relationship with books; I love reading books, they are my refuge and solace, my joy and delight. The best friends that I have in life are books and the adventures they have taken me on.

On this journey of self-discovery, my mom has played a very integral part by introducing me to religion where I got to know Jesus and all about his adventure. Just before she passed away, she left me in the hands of a profound teacher. In a way, she left me with a teacher I would come to love, to fear, to avoid, to want, to desire. This is my wife. My wife has been like a catalyst which expedites a particular action towards its onward journey. The learning that I have gone through in the last 6 years pales in comparison to the 34 years before that. It is like a sort of distinct phase learning.

The first 34 years were devoted to being born, study, read, drink, smoke, make money in that order. All through that phase, my Mom silently watched me. I know sometimes she must have felt I was a lost soul, especially when I was drinking too much. I call this Phase 1.

What's occurred in the last 6 years is a giant leap in my life. The leap has not been made in one single jump. It has been like you jumping on a trampoline — Up and down, the more force you come down with the more higher you go the higher you go the broader your vision. This is Phase 2 of my life.

My Personal Teachers

By Phase 2, I am referring to the last 6 years of my married life, which thankfully still lasts today. There were times when I wanted to avoid the learning but I knew that there was only one way to live life and that is through it. I cannot ignore what life teaches me through my wife. My wife brought a change to my life, which till she arrived, was involved working hard, making money, friends and drinking. Sometimes, the drinking was hard. The drinking hard part really hit a sad note because it continued well into the marriage. To say the least, it did not help much.

She was not always the way I see her now; because I did not understand the importance of her presence in my life. I kept doing things which I assumed were most important to her. I did not pause long enough to care deeply about her language of love. I was too full of myself and assumed a lot. The few things that I assumed were: I was making enough money to sustain a family, we have a home back in India, we have a kid who can go to a good school, we have a decent house to live in, and good food on the table, my time out with the family during the break times, and so on and so forth. With all this going on, I felt confident that everything was just fine. Actually, with all this going on, nothing seemed to be fine. Like a dormant volcano, once in a while, there would be an eruption. This would lead to a long cooling off period.

Initially I just put all the blame on her shoulders. My reasoning was that I did not have any of these issues until we were married. The only variable was being married, so it goes without saying that she had to take the blame. There were moments we came frighteningly close to talking about separating. As I was playing out the drama of being the best husband, father and a great person, I continued defending my position in life and started gathering support for myself. I wanted the universe to prove me right and her wrong. Peace was not a word which featured in our lives.

I resisted every effort she was making for me to see life as it was. The more I resisted, the more I kept attracting the same old routine. The dormant volcano was now a full-fledged active one.

I feel remorse and sorry for the times I made her really sad by my ego-driven reasoning. But this remorse was short-lived. It was during this time of turmoil that my search within myself intensified. If you think I gave up drinking, so I could be sober during my search, you are wrong. This did not happen till I completed my first Vipassana session. I think life decided to hurry up and bring me my lessons forward rather than make my wife suffer. The old seeds that were buried started to take root. I re-read Tony Demello's books, and then, Eckhart Tolle's *Power of Now*. I looked for help through books as they have been one of my best teachers. I found Gary Chapman's book on relationships. Now, I had all the theory and I got to work. Again, I made the fundamental mistake that most of us do as amateurs. I thought I should apply all the knowledge, theory and learning on my wife instead of on me. This was because I still did not get it. I was hard-wired to my left-brained thinking — I believed in the OUTSIDE IN theory and practice because that was the experience that I always had. I had only seen this in my limited reality. I was because I did things. I was a solutions man; a project manager. I was the one who made things happen.

Don't get me wrong, outside it works. It is real. It gets fatally flawed when you start relying and believing that it is the only way of living. During this period, I knew the theory inside out; I had the knowledge. I had read enough to understand the meaning of the words. What I lacked was the wisdom. I was missing the key link. I had not experienced the meaning of the words. It was like this — I understood through reading and knowledge how a fruit should look like, taste like, feel like, smell like. What was I missing? I had never tasted a fruit, that's all. And this was making the whole difference.

To get it, I needed to learn some more lessons. These were hard knocks in the school of life. My wife moved to India with our son for some time. We thought this would help. It did not. We tried being silent for a while. It did not help. We tried coming mid-way to bridge the gap, found that this too was not working. Just like that, one day I got it. In a way, I tasted the fruit. It was the proverbial "coin-dropping" moment...

It was never ever about my wife. It was all about me! A-ha! It had always been about me. I didn't need to 'fix' her. I simply had to sit back and observe myself. When I did this, my interpretation of life changed completely. I realised all that I said I was doing for my wife, kid and the family were really for myself. I was selfish and kept blaming her for being selfish. It only takes a moment to learn. I think Learning is always in the moment never in the past or future.

After this moment, it was as though I had got rid of my coloured glasses. I saw my wife in a new light. Literally, there was more light around her. The light was always there; it was my glasses that kept me from noticing. It pays to change the glasses, trust me. That is when I saw that she was here to facilitate and hasten my learning; she was here to propel me upward towards the light — the light where I could take time to become more intimate with myself, my thoughts, my passions, my purpose. It was then that I saw clearly that my first passion at this moment was awareness followed by family. A couple of years ago, the time and attention I was giving to these two passions was negligible. So I turned it around. This is wealth creation in the truest sense. Paying attention to your relationships and listening to the lessons they are trying to teach.

Just before you finish, have a go at your present reality and take this is a jump-off point towards a successful life.

Where are you and where do you want to go?

This circle of perspective is like an expanding spiral. Start from the centre of the circle and move out one step at a time. At this point in time, let's just concentrate on the 7 major areas of life. These are:

- Mind
- Body
- Spiritual
- Professional
- Financial
- Emotional
- Relations

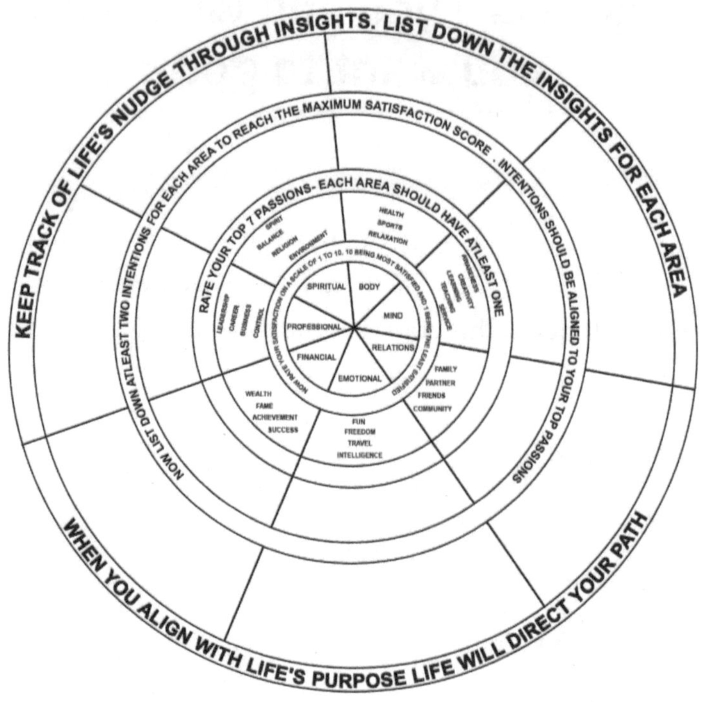

1. Start with the centre point of the circle and move outwards. Assign a score to each of the areas mentioned above from 0 to 10-Zero being the least satisfied and 10 being the most satisfied.
2. What is the satisfaction level of your relationships?
3. How much time are you giving to nurture them?
4. How much attention are you giving your relationships so that they grow abundantly?

5. What are the 3 actions you can take to balance the relationship score with the highest of the other areas?

Paying attention and giving time to relationships is how you develop them. If this is not a major area of your life, pause now and take a look around you. Relationships not only to your immediate beings around you, take time to understand the depth of your relationship with yourself? How much do you love yourself? Love's two visible arms are the time you spend and the attention you give.

Awareness, the first key, which is handed down on day one means to pay attention, focused attention. This act alone is enough for you to start mending any deformed relationships. It also opens up your vision to see the lesson each relationship has in store for you.

When you pay close attention over a period of time then you can see that relationships are your best teachers. They are your source for inspiration and living fully. The first step in changing the external connections is to get to know yourself. To know yourself you will have to spend time going inward, within, in silence with gratitude to life for giving you this human experience.

Once you come to the same realisation that I came to "it is not her, or they, or him, but is I." Once you have this refreshing experience life will change. This change will be beyond some of your most daring and adventurous imagination. Go for it.

If you are unable to list down 3 actions, you are going to take to get more intimate with yourself I suggest you take a moment to ask yourself if you really want to know yourself. If the answer is Yes, life will take you to the next step without your intervention. Trust life and flow with it

This one technique of meditation is the key to 80% of your success in life. Spend 20% of your day in mediation and self-care to reap the benefits.

May all beings be Happy!

— THE END —

Reference

1. **You can check out my Yoga Guru's website here at**: http://www.sohamyogastudio.org/new_aboutus.php
2. http://www.dayblocks.com or http://download.cnet.com/Vision-Board-Builder/3000–2192_4–75313237.html
3. http://www.xmind.net/m/Grf4
4. **Check out** http://www.suhastalwar.com/#fire_walk
5. **You might want to read the complete version** here http://communicate.eckharttolle.com/news/2012/01/24/eckhart-on-presence-the-law-of-attraction/
6. http://www.amazon.in/Passion-Test-Effortless-Discovering-Purpose/dp/0452289858/ref=sr_1_1?ie=UTF8&qid=1469772056&sr=8–1&keywords=the+passion+test
7. https://thepassiontest.geniusu.com/
8. Check out https://www.projectsmart.co.uk/smart-goals.php.
9. http://www.nlpu.com/NewDesign/NLPU_WhatIsNLP.html

Here are some interesting and useful links

5 steps to create powerful intentions http://www.chopra.com/ccl/5-steps-to-setting-powerful-intentions

3 ways to focus your intentions http://intention-focus.com/focus-intention

imagine focus feel http://tinybuddha.com/blog/the-power-of-focus-directing-your-life-with-intention/

10. http://365grateful.com/.
11. http://www.happify.com/hd/the-science-behind-gratitude/
12. https://www.ted.com/talks/david_steindl_rast_want_to_be_happy_be_grateful?language=en
13. **The "unstuck blog"** https://www.unstuck.com/gratitude/gives 9 influential gratitude cards.
14. **Prepare "your list"** http://goinswriter.com/thankful/
15. **The change blog** http://www.thechangeblog.com/gratitude/

100 day gratitude challenge https://grandeurvision.wordpress.com/100-day-gratitude-challenge/

5 tips to happier life http://www.positivityblog.com/index.php/2015/09/30/gratitude-tips/

Tiny Buddha's Practice gratitude to change your life http://tinybuddha.com/blog/how-to-start-a-gratitude-practice-to-change-your-life/

Gratitude Log http://www.gratitudelog.com/